MISSION AS TRANSFORMATION
LEARNING FROM CATALYSTS

Series Preface

While we delight to serve the academic community, our mission is to enable the global church to engage more readily in God's mission in its very diverse contexts. To do this we seek to bring practitioners and academics together. Our desire is that this series will bridge the gap that sometimes exists between, on the one hand, Christian leaders and mission practitioners and, on the other, Christian researchers.

About the Editors

David Cranston is a consultant surgeon and senior lecturer in the Nuffield Department of Surgical Sciences in the University of Oxford, a Governing Body Fellow at Green Templeton College Oxford and a Licenced Lay Minister in the Church of England. He has been Chairman of the OCMS Executive Committee since 2010.

Ruth Padilla DeBorst currently serves as Director of Christian Formation and Leadership Development with World Vision International. As a board member of the Latin American Theological Fellowship she is tasked to serve on the Networking Team of INFEMIT. She shares parenting of their blended, multi-cultural family with her husband, James Padilla DeBorst, and community life with the members of Casa Adobe, in Costa Rica.

MISSION AS TRANSFORMATION
LEARNING FROM CATALYSTS

Edited by
David Cranston and
Ruth Padilla DeBorst

First published 2013 by Regnum Books International in partnership with
International Fellowship for Mission as Transformation (INFMIT)
Apartado 349-1002, San José, Costa Rica
www.infemit.org

Regnum is an imprint of the Oxford Centre for Mission Studies
St. Philip and St. James Church, Woodstock Road, Oxford, OX2 6HR, UK
www.ocms.ac.uk/regnum

09 08 07 06 05 04 03 8 7 6 5 4 3 2 1

British Library Cataloguing in Publication Data
A catalogue record for this book is available from the British Library

ISBN: 978-1-506477-76-3

Typeset in Palatino by WORDS BY DESIGN
Cover design by WORDS BY DESIGN

The 2012 Forum and the publication of this book has been made possible through a friend of OCMS who wishes to remain anonymous.

The paper used for the text of this book Forest Stewardship Council (FSC) Certified

Distributed by 1517 Media in the US and Canada

Dedication

To the thousands of unrecognized
heroes of transformational mission all over the world.

CONTENTS

INTRODUCTION

'As you sent me into the world, I have sent them into the world' (John 17.18). This was Jesus' prayer to God for his followers. What does it mean to be sent as Jesus into the world? What should that look like in the current world scene? How are followers of Jesus to live out God's mission in particular, local contexts? Questions of radical discipleship like these were at the heart of the movement that brought together theologian practitioners from around the world during the 1980s as the International Fellowship of Evangelical Mission Theologians (INFEMIT). This movement gave birth to the Oxford Centre for Mission Studies (OCMS) in 1983. Its purpose, in the words of Chris Sugden, was 'to address the potential drain of leadership in the churches of the Global South through postgraduate studies in the West'. By opening opportunities through OCMS for research and scholarship, validated by recognized educational institutions, INFEMIT sought, as Al Tizon explains, 'to tackle a range of contemporary theological and socio-political issues in a distinctively transformational key for the worldwide missionary community, but especially for Two Third World Churches engaged in mission in their particular contexts'. The first two Executive Directors of OCMS were Vinay Samuel and Chris Sugden. In 2007, Wonsuk Ma succeeded them and under his leadership, by God's grace, OCMS has continued to grow as a community of world scholars who seek to live as Jesus in the world.

The academic programmes, publications and seminars have always been at the core of OCMS's service to mission circles. The Council and Executive Committee continue to be committed to engage in discussion around cutting-edge mission topics, in order to strengthen the mission of Christian communities in their contexts. It is this commitment that moved the Council of Trustees to approve the development of an annual consultation with the name *Stott -Bediako Forum on the Gospel and the World Today* to be hosted annually by OCMS in co-operation with INFEMIT, now known as the International Fellowship for Mission as Transformation.

Why entitle these annual consultations the 'Stott Bediako Forum'? Well, because in the council's view, perhaps no two individuals embody the aims of this Forum more completely than these two followers of Jesus Christ, John Stott and Kwame Bediako.

John Stott lived a rich life of 90 years and died on 27th July 2011. His support and encouragement of the worldwide church through teaching, preaching and writing are well known. His legacy is beautifully portrayed in the paper by Monty Barker. John Stott was a great supporter of OCMS and in 2008 wrote:

> *The Oxford Centre for Mission Studies (OCMS) is an organization with which I have been involved since its inception in 1983, and I have watched its development with great satisfaction. I am delighted to have this opportunity to commend its work to you for your prayerful and financial support. It is the conviction of OCMS, which I share, that during this century many of the influential leaders in the church will come from the Global South. The ongoing work of OCMS in preparing many of them for leadership, through its postgraduate and research programmes, will be a key part in this process.*

Kwame Bediako lived most of his life in his native Ghana and died in June 2008. Kwabena Asamoah-Gyadu explores his life and contribution to the mission of the church. Of Bediako, Chris Wright, director of Langham Partnership International, wrote:

> *Kwame was one of the most remarkable senior African leaders I have ever met. He had a surpassing level of scholarship (two doctorates – one in English and one in French). He had a range of knowledge of the history of the church in Africa (and Europe) that could keep us spellbound for hours just listening to his stories. And he had a most profound understanding of the relationship between the gospel and African culture. He also had a huge passion to bring African Christians together to affirm their Christian identity in authentic ways that would overcome some of the worst legacies of the colonial era. And yet he wore all this learning with such a light touch. His twinkling eyes and sparkling humour and laughter were a constant tonic. It has been such a joy and privilege to know him for many years. It is hard at a time like this to understand the ways of the Lord. But the legacy that Kwame Bediako leaves is simply enormous.*

This book is the product of the first Stott-Bediako Forum, held in 2012 with the title 'Portraits of Catalysts'. The aim of this particular Forum was to learn from the stories of Christian leaders whose lives and work have served as catalysts for transformation as each, in his or her particular way, facilitated the intersection between the Good News of Jesus Christ and the context in which they lived, and in particular amongst people who are suffering. The purpose was *not* to construct a list of 'who's who' in transformational mission, but simply to offer insights into the life of a number of well known and lesser known followers of Christ of recent decades and from around the world.

The studies in this edited volume are not intended to glorify the individuals themselves, for the wish of all of them would be that Christ, and Christ alone, be glorified. The portraits do, however, invite us to witness God's work in and through men and a woman who, by God's grace, effected transformation both locally and globally. Our expectation is that by entering into their life stories and theological experiences, and by exploring their reading and living out the gospel, readers will be inspired to engage yet more intentionally in God's mission in God's world.

We invite you now to enjoy learning from the two humble and prolific followers of Jesus after whom the Forum is named, John Stott and Kwame Bediako, and from the other catalysts of transformation here portrayed, Peter Kuzmic, Ron Sider, David Bussau, Juan José Barreda, Catharine Padilla, and David Gitari. We trust that, as we learn together, Jesus' prayer for us may become a reality: May we be sent as Jesus was into the world!

David Cranston and Ruth Padilla DeBorst

JOHN STOTT
HE WROTE FOR MILLIONS, PREACHED TO THOUSANDS, BUT INVESTED IN INDIVIDUALS

MONTY BARKER

Monty Barker is a retired consultant psychiatrist and past chairman of the executive board of OCMS. A licensed lay minister in the Anglican Church, he regularly teaches at the Union Biblical Seninary in Pune, India.

At the memorial service for John Stott, in January 2012, in St Paul's Cathedral, in central London, the words which seemed to me to sum up John Stott's life and ministry were those of a Jewish follower of Jesus, Mark Greene, the director of the London Institute for Contemporary Christianity when he declared:

John Stott wrote for millions, preached to thousands, but invested in individuals.

Few really knew him as a person. Many heard him preach but multitudes still read him as an author.

WHO WAS JOHN STOTT?

I first came across John Stott's name in 1954. I was in a church in London and came across a little book called *Men with a Message.* I began to read it and the clarity, the depth and the breadth of this writer, of whom I had never heard, electrified me. I bought it for a shilling. I still have it, and keep it as one of those books which began my acquaintance with John Stott.

In the late 1950's, I heard him as a student and listened to many of his talks. At one conference, John Stott and Martyn Lloyd-Jones were both speaking. Lloyd-Jones was the more charismatic preacher but I remember how carefully crafted John Stott's talks were. In the 1970's, I shared a platform with John from time to time; I was the practical guy, but it was John who lifted the heart up to heaven.

I could never call myself a close friend, but his writing had a profound impact on me. Yet, this man who influenced the lives of millions, was never a Canon of St Paul's Cathedral, as were his successors at All Soul's Church; John Stott was never a member of the Church of England Synod; he was never a Bishop although he was an advisor to so many. In ecclesiastical terms, he was a nobody. If you look at him at one level, he never 'made it'. Yet Time magazine named him as one of the most significant figures of the twentieth century, along with such people as Bill Gates. One of John Stott's contemporaries was David Edwards, a man with a formidable intellect who was on the liberal side of the Church of England. He was no fan of John's preaching or his theology, but he said that, 'apart from William Temple (a former Archbishop of Canterbury), John Stott was the most influential clergyman of the twentieth century.'

Adrian Hastings, Professor of Theology in Leeds University, a historian of both the Church of England and global Christianity, said that John Stott 'must be counted one of the most influential Christian figures in the world'.

John Stott would have seen himself primarily as an Anglican evangelical. Anglican because that was the church in which he was born and brought up and with which he wished to remain associated but evangelical because this was integral to authentic Christianity. He said he was:

Under scripture and under grace.
Sola scriptura sola gratia

Submission to scripture and submission at the foot of the cross of Christ were at the heart of his life and ministry.

In a famous dialogue with David Edwards, he said 'You see, the difference between us, David, can be summed up in the discussion between Luther and Erasmus. For, as Luther said to Erasmus, you sit above scripture and judge it, whereas I sit under scripture and let it judge me'.

John Stott's Background

John Stott was born in 1921 in Harley Street, one of the most prestigious streets in London. At the age of eight, he was sent away to boarding school. He then went on to Rugby, one of the leading schools of its kind in England and from where the game of rugby originated. He was a prize-winner, a sportsman and he became head boy. Rugby was also where he became a Christian, at the age of 17 in 1938.

After leaving school, he went to Cambridge University, where from 1940-1945, he was a student in Trinity College. He was so disciplined that other people felt almost inhibited and wretched in comparison to him. A fellow student at that time said, 'Everything he did related to Christ, it was so discouraging! But then we were able to have a good laugh with him and realized he was human after all!'

I had the privilege of staying with him on one occasion in the Rectory, colloquially known as the 'Stottery'. I was in a room at the top of the house, and breakfast was at the bottom of the house. One had to go back to the top after breakfast to clean one's teeth. It was very different from my Scottish background. The breakfast was sumptuous, whereas I was used to porridge! Everyone read the paper at table; in my home you never read in the company of others – meals were times for conversation. John asked as I came down for breakfast, 'would you like a newspaper?' I said 'no thank you', but he still opened his and started reading it. After breakfast, we went into the drawing room and knelt down for prayers against the settee with its silk brocade and prayed together. It was quite an experience. A different world – and yet he was a man who had the most profound influence on my life.

Even as a curate, John had an eye for the poor, for the outsider, and for the disadvantaged. He noticed the poor in the parish of All Souls, and he put the clubhouse into operation for those who would never darken the door of the church.

In 1950, he became Rector and he undertook his first major mission at Cambridge University in 1952. In 1954, the Bishop of London asked him to write a book for Lent for the diocese that was published under the title *Men with a Message.* Then followed *Basic Christianity,* in 1958, probably his most widely read book. In 1970, he felt his ministry at All Souls should be shared with another person so that he could be freed for a wider ministry and Michael Baughen joined as vicar (later becoming Bishop of Chester) while John remained as Rector.

It was during these years that he began to think about other projects. These involved helping scholars from overseas to come for postgraduate research, and supplying literature at low cost to pastors around the world. So began the Langham scholarships and the Evangelical Literature Trust.

He continued with his teaching ministry, his writing ministry, and his university missions throughout the world and, in 1974, was co-chairman with Billy Graham of the first Lausanne Congress on World Evangelism.

He became Rector Emeritus of All Souls in 1975 and increased his global ministry, becoming Uncle John to so many people throughout the world. During this time, he founded the London Institute for Contemporary Christianity with the aim of gathering together professional men and women and helping them to study together on how to live as Christians in every part of their lives, seven days a week, whether as a doctor or journalist or teacher or politician.

He was invested with a Lambeth doctorate, and by then had had the offer of several bishoprics, which he turned down. In 1998, health issues forced him to give up driving and, in 2001, he asked Chris Wright to succeed him as director of the Langham Trust which subsequently became the Langham Partnership International. In that year, he was made a CBE (Commander of the British Empire) for services as chaplain to the Queen and his ministry to the global church.

In 2007, he moved to St Barnabas College in East Grinstead, a care home with an Anglo-Catholic heritage. The care was outstanding and he coped after a fashion with the prevailing tradition but he was not totally at home with it. That year, he gave his last public sermon at the Keswick Convention. He asked to stand for it and managed to do so holding on so grimly, that his hands had to be prized away, which was sad but in a way a wonderful sight. He had no fear or dying although he was slightly apprehensive of the process and certainly did not want doctors to strive officiously to keep him alive for he knew that he had something wonderful waiting for him.

He came from a privileged background. Yet for 30 years he lived over a stable block in two rooms in Bridford Mews behind his previous rectory. He made a lot of money from his books but lived frugally, using his money to found the Langham Trust. He was brought up in an elitist situation but he refused consideration for a bishopric. He was exceptionally gifted but those gifts were not used to his own advantage but to the advantage of others whose gifts he could foster. He had a father who was knighted for his services to medicine and to his country in the First World War but he chose to read theology after obtaining a first in French at Cambridge.

He did not live up to his father's expectations of him, not least in refusing the call to fight in the Second World War, when he became a conscientious objector. Perhaps that was something of an adolescent rebellion and John would say in his later years that he wished he had had someone to encourage a more reasoned approach at that time. His father would have liked him to go into the civil service, or the colonial service but he did take one thing from his father, and that was a love of ornithology (bird watching) that remained to the end of his days. He often encouraged others to follow his love of birds 'For', as he said, 'the Lord told us, consider the birds of the air and learn from them'. He shared his love in one of his later books, *The Birds our Teachers* and many people caught something of his passion for ornithology.

JOHN STOTT'S MENTORS

John Stott had a number of mentors. Eric Nash was the first. Eric Nash was employed by the Scripture Union and he had a burden for able young men coming from so-called public schools (which are actually private fee-paying schools) and wealthy backgrounds, who he felt could have a real influence if they became Christians. He ran camps for these people and John Stott was one such. A friend commented about Nash that 'he showed John the loveliness of Christ, and John never lost sight of that vision'. Nash did not just bring him to Christ, but also wrote letters to him after, when he left school, on a daily and later weekly basis, to encourage him and nurse him through his early days as a Christian.

Oliver Barclay was another influence on his life. He is one of those unsung leaders of the church of whom few have heard. A brilliant man who, after finishing his Ph.D., gave his life to encouraging students. He became General Secretary of what was then the Inter Varsity Fellowship (IVF), now called the Universities and Colleges Christian Fellowship (UCCF). Oliver Barclay did not tell students what to do; rather he would say, 'we need to have a chin wag' (an upper class way of saying 'let's have a chat'). He would take students for a walk and say 'there's another group doing so and so' which was his way of saying I think you ought to think of doing this. But he would never say it directly. Talking of John Stott, he said of their Cambridge days together, 'There was one person who was such a wonderful witness that we couldn't put him on committee. His gifts would have been wasted spending time on committees'.

Another important influence on John Stott was Dr. Douglas Johnson. Known as DJ, he was the great strategist of evangelicalism. Not many people have heard of him either for, like Oliver Barclay, he wanted to remain in the background. When Douglas Johnson was a medical student he arranged to be in three medical schools during the course of his studies, and while he was learning anatomy and pathology and physiology, he would witness and talk about Christ. Christian unions began in those three universities. He allowed students to make mistakes. He realized that if one tried to push them around they would rebel. DJ was probably one of the prime movers of the International Fellowship for Evangelical students (IFES). When the possibility of becoming a bishop in Australia first came up, DJ was the one who said to John; 'Be careful, I think you are of more value where you are now in All Souls than you would be in Australia. If I was the archangel Gabriel in charge of heavenly postings, I would certainly keep you in Langham Place.'

It was DJ who introduced him to the life of Charles Simeon, of whom John said, 'He was something of a guru to me'. Charles Simeon (1759-1836) was the vicar of Holy Trinity Church, Cambridge, for 54 years and his ministry was built on submission to everything that scripture taught, including those things that are difficult to reconcile. He said that the truth lies neither at one extreme nor the other, nor in a confused mixture of both, but in both extremes held together in tension, even if we may find that difficult to comprehend.

There were tremendous similarities between Charles Simeon and John Stott. They were both bachelors living in the same place for decades and remaining in the same church throughout their lives. They had a love for students and a ministry to them. They had a worldwide outlook: Charles Simeon was the one who helped found the Church Mission to the Jews and the Church Missionary Society, while having a deep social concern at the same time. Reading the biography of Charles Simeon helps one to understand something of the stable from which John Stott came.

John Stott's Legacy

Oliver Barclay said, 'Something new was brought to life through the evangelism of John Stott. He was Biblical; he was scholarly but not academic; he was firm but not caustic. He was a man with a more evident love for people than some of the old missioners and preachers.'

The impact of his missions in the 1950s was probably greater than anything that had been seen since 1900. This was a new kind of evangelism, thoughtful and aware, yet not ignoring apologetics or theology. He could speak to the theology of others with sympathy as well as with biblical authority. His addresses at the university missions formed the framework of his book *Basic Christianity* and brought many people into the kingdom in those years.

There were other events happening in Britain in the 1950's. Billy Graham first came to Harringay in 1954 and John Stott, among others, encouraged him when he was not sure if he could cope with England. His Crusade had a remarkable effect on the churches and theological colleges up and down the country. It also led to a friendship between Billy Graham and John Stott, which resulted in the first Congress for World Evangelism in Lausanne in 1974, 20 years later. The friendship that had developed emboldened John Stott to withstand pressures from North America, which needed to be resisted as churches in developing countries felt that evangelism must be associated with social engagement. The Langham Partnership grew out of this move towards holistic mission and the Oxford Centre for Mission Studies also was deeply influenced by John Stott's embrace of this new direction.

Within the Church of England, John Stott revived the Eclectic Society that had been founded by John Newton in 1793. This was a group of young men in ministry who met to share fellowship together. Charles Simeon continued this and sometimes the men were encouraged to bring their wives, of whom he said: 'In my ministers' meetings I also have the ministresses, by far and away the better halves'. There were echoes of Simeon when a Bishop said to me a few years ago before the days of women vicars: 'I invite the wives to accompany their husbands to clergy conferences; it earths them and they behave much better!'

John Stott's Writings

John Stott was a prolific author. 50 books came from his pen. His first book *Men with a Message* was commissioned by the Bishop of London who said, 'This little book shows the intellectual basis upon which an especially busy priest builds his parish life and work'.

John felt that there was no greater need than that we should allow our minds to be conditioned and our lives to be reformed by the word of God.

That was at the heart of his writing but it was his preaching that led to his writing. It was his mission talks that led to *Basic Christianity*. He was intent that this work on which he laboured and struggled – as he did also over the book which summed up the heart of the gospel that he preached, *The Cross of Christ* – should also be put into print. Unlike some others. he did not just give a talk and then hand it to the printers. He would hone it and it would go through his brain a second time before it went through his pen.

One book he wrote was called *Essentials*. It followed the debate with David Edwards, when he rose to the challenge of being prepared to be questioned and face questions in public.

Issues facing Christians Today is to my mind one of his best books. He prepared what he thought the Bible said on different issues, such as global poverty, ethnic diversity, ecology, sexuality and the world of work. Then he would preach it to a group of representative people, in the latter case business tycoons, unemployed men, someone who was retired, someone who was redundant, as well as people in work. He would listen to their response and re-write it and finally it was published as a book. Now in its fourth edition, it is superb, bringing together scripture with issues in the modern world. He would listen to the word of God but also listen to the parish, to the press, to the journalists, and to what else was going on. This idea of double listening came from Spurgeon who used to speak of the need to have 'the Bible in one hand and the newspaper in the other'.

The Bible speaks Today series was a remarkable venture. He first wrote on Galatians, and Martyn Lloyd-Jones said of this very lucid commentary, that 'John told Paul what he should have written rather than what he actually said'! That is a bit ungenerous, but nevertheless there may be an element of truth in it. There were other contributions and several other contributors to the series said how John made very helpful editorial comments such as 'I think this might be better if it was put in this way' or 'do you think it would be more helpful if' rather than 'you should write this'.

He introduced the whole series by saying 'these expositions have a three-fold aim: to expound the biblical text, to relate it to contemporary life, and to be readable. There is nothing more necessary for the life, growth and health of the churches than they should hear and read what the Spirit is saying to them through the ancient text.'

Bishop Holloway of Edinburgh was asked by the Church Times to review John's exposition of the Sermon on the Mount, '*Christian Counter Culture*' and he said, as he read it on the train going from London to Edinburgh:

> *There I was on a high speed retreat led by John Stott, and like a lot of contemporary writers on the Bible, John Stott's intention is to let the Bible speak to us and to confront us by the Sermon on the Mount in a fresh and personal way without shirking critical issues. In this he has succeeded admirably. Reading the book was a salutary shock to me because like many people who like to be thought progressive and up to date I have been a little soft centred when it comes to dealing with personal morality, though less so in the area of institutional morality. I need to be acquainted with the absolute standard of the holiness of Christ in private as well as in public behaviour.*

Again, in referring to the discussion with David Edwards, it was Holloway who said in the Church Times: 'David Edwards wants to make us think. John Stott wants to make us holy. We need to hear both challenges but John Stott's is the primary one'.

John Stott gave himself to others. He loved people. He wrote letters to them in handwriting that was always legible. The letters were often short, always to the point and elegant. Many Christian leaders have spoken or written of what John Stott meant to them, and often it was in his writing and in remembering things about them: in words of comfort and encouragement; sometimes in a closing prayer, sometimes in a passing comment, a balm to the soul. One scholar, dilatory in finishing his Ph.D., received a letter from John who had written a most gracious but compelling jolt to this person telling him to 'Get on with it'!

John gave himself in varying degrees to so many, but when it came to asking things of others and sharing himself with others, it was only with a few. He had his feet of clay and that gives one the feeling that if God could use him maybe he can use me too. He knew what it was to suffer, to struggle and to have doubts. He did have outbursts of impatience and one saw this sometimes when he was tired in a quick answer to a question that was not so much an answer as a put down. And he had a rigidity that could seem ungracious at times. But like Caleb at 85 and even beyond the age of 85, his mind was active and he had no wish to be discounted because of his age.

Yes, there was a distance in him sometimes, a formality. He seldom spoke about singleness or sex or dependency or loneliness or indeed his last five years in a nursing home with outstanding care but a high church tradition with which he was not particularly comfortable.

His four last books were more personal. In *Calling Christian Leaders,* he attacks the culture, including his own culture. In *The Living Church,* he speaks of the need to love one's congregation. In *The Radical Disciple,* he admitted weeping over his own dependency. In his Keswick address, *The Last Word,* there is a section where he speaks of the renunciations of his life, marriage, academia, and hierarchy and yet in all those renunciations, God richly rewarded him with other things.

It was Africans who were the best, along with his friends in Latin America, at breaking through his reserve. He loved Africans. They did not allow him to remain British, imprisoned in a tie, jacket and collar. Their joy and their effervescence swept him along, perhaps even allowing his knees to bend a little and his arms to float a little in singing and worship.

He had his chosen friends, his faults and his struggles – but what was it that really made him tick? Well, it is there on his gravestone in Dale, near his Welsh home, The Hookses. It was his love for Christ, his desire to be like him and his aim to share Him with others.

Buried here are the ashes of
JOHN R.W.STOTT
(1921-2011)
Rector of All Souls Church
Langham Place, London
1950-1975
Rector Emeritus 1975-2011
Who resolved
Both as the ground of his salvation
And as the subject of his ministry
To know nothing except
JESUS CHRIST
And him crucified

(1 Corinthians 2:2)

KWAME BEDIAKO 'MR AFRICAN THEOLOGY'

J. KWABENA ASAMOAH-GYADU

J. Kwabena Asamoah-Gyadu is Professor of Contemporary African Christianity and Pentecostal-Charismatic Studies at the Trinity Theological Seminary at Legon in Accra, Ghana.

KWAME BEDIAKO'S LEGACY

The invitation to write a paper in memory of Kwame Bediako offers the opportunity to reiterate what we have lost in Kwame Bediako, who was an outstanding African pastor, teacher and theologian, and whose legacy – consisting of thoughts, actions, writings and influences – is still with us, and will continue to shape theological thought in Africa and beyond for many years to come. He worked to train a new generation of theologians – African and Western – who are open to learn in and from Africa. To that end, Andrew F. Walls, a doyen of the study of Christianity in Africa and himself Bediako's teacher, mentor and close friend, was correct when he concluded in an article on Bediako's legacy:

> *[Bediako's] all too few writings will continue their influence, as will his institute's* Journal of African Christian Thought, *to which he so often contributed. There are other books that he never completed, rich material lying in those electrifying lecture courses and biblical expositions. But much of his finest work has been written in the lives and thinking of his students, colleagues, and friends, and in the concept of the institution he founded, and in the networks he helped to establish, enhance, and maintain. It is a rich legacy, much of it prudently invested for future use (Walls 2008:193).*

I also 'as one untimely born', to borrow from Pauline discourse on his apostolic calling, worked with Kwame Bediako as a seminary intern between 1985 and 1987. Within the period, he was also my teacher in Comparative Religions. Our relationship continued from there as he gradually co-opted me into his circle of young friends and proposed my name as the West Africa sub-regional co-ordinator of the African

Theological Fellowship. My experience with Kwame Bediako was that he constantly planted in those who studied under him the thought that firstly Christian theological scholarship must always engage with contextual issues. Secondly, that it must always be seen as a form of ministry in its own right; and thirdly, that 'African theology was not an exotic minority specialization but an essential component in a developing global discourse' (Walls 2008:193). He showed great interest in primal religions and their relation to Christianity. These religions, in the words of Walls, were primal in the sense of pre-dating the so called world religions. Kwame Bediako often said and wrote that throughout Christian history, 'they have proved the most fertile soil for the Christian message, so that they form the background, the substructure…of the faith of a high percentage of the world's Christians and influence their worldview' (Walls 2008:190).

Kwame Bediako was a scholar with an exceptional pedigree, a forceful writer, and a very powerful and evangelically passionate preacher. From July 1987, Kwame Bediako was the Alexander Duff Visiting Lecturer in the Centre of the Study of Christianity in the Non-Western World at New College, University of Edinburgh. Between 1986 and 1998 he taught in Edinburgh as a Visiting Scholar in African Christianity and served as advisor to several research students whose work testifies to his memory as a great thinker of our generation. Bediako was also invited to give the first Professor O.G. Myklebust Memorial Lecture in 2005, which marked the centenary of the birth of the founder of missiology as a theological discipline in Norway. Thus, he served the course of African Christianity and beyond. In 2008, Kwame Bediako was awarded an honorary doctorate on the occasion of the centenary anniversary of the MF Norwegian School of Theology. It would not surprise those who knew the breadth and depth of his theological mind that at least three Ph.D. research projects have already been completed on his work in reputable institutions around the world. This includes Roar G. Fortland's doctoral dissertation 'Ancestor Christology in Context – Theological Perspectives of Kwame Bediako' written for the MF Norwegian School of Theology in 2005.

BEDIAKO: HIS LIFE AND MINISTRY

It is said among the Akan of Ghana that 'it is only at the demise of the frog that its actual length comes to be known.' At his funeral, the world came to know that Kwame, as everybody called him, was actually born as Manasseh Kwame Darkwa Bediako. His father was Ephraim Nkansah Bediako and his mother, Selina Duodu. They hailed from Agona Nsaba, an early Presbyterian Mission stronghold, in the Central Region. He grew up at the Accra Police Depot, where his father was a police inspector. Bediako had his secondary education at a Methodist mission school, Mfantsipim, or as its old students would have it, 'The School' to underscore its place as the earliest and best boys' school in Ghana. Those who have been associated with Mfantsipim speak proudly of the international achievements of its old boys, including the former Secretary General of the United Nations, Kofi Annan, who was a few years ahead of Bediako.

Kwame Bediako is described as an exceptional student with great oratorical skills by his friends from Mfantsipim School (Funeral Tribute 2008:22-23). Kwame's very dark complexion was striking, and apparently because of that his classmates nicknamed him 'Joe Noir' or 'Joe Flash'. Kwame served as Head Prefect of 'The School' and proceeded from there to study French at the University of Ghana, where he obtained a scholarship to continue his studies in France. He gained his Masters and Ph.D. degrees in French Literature and African Literature in French at the University of Bordeaux. However, before the end of his studies, Kwame, who was then a self-confessed atheist, underwent a radical transformation in life that is comparable to the experience of Paul on the road to Damascus. He came to believe and exercise personal faith in the Lord Jesus Christ.

Conversion to Christ, Marriage and Theological Studies

Before Kwame left for France in 1969, his father, as a number of Africans still do today, had taken his son's name to a shrine so that he would be protected from evil spirits, witches and relations who may be envious of a rare opportunity to study abroad. Kwame himself became an atheist having imbibed French existentialist philosophies, and he actively disputed Christian claims with Christian students until the Lord intervened in his life in 1970. In the bath one day – and he told the story several times – 'the fact that Christ is the Truth, the integrating principle of life as well as the key to true intellectual coherence, for himself and for the whole world, was impressed upon him with irresistible force' (Visser and Bediako 2000: vii-viii). The radical nature of his conversion experience nearly led him to abandon his studies in French in favour of active evangelism. This was a step that had been taken by a number of people in Ghana at the time. The urge to preach Christ in expectation of the *parousia* led several known African university students to abandon their studies and evangelize for Christ. Kwame was prevailed upon to stay the course but, as it turned out, he eventually came to 'recognize scholarship as itself a missionary vocation' (Walls 2008:189).

In the programme for his funeral, Bediako's family inserted a beautiful picture showing him wearing a Ghanaian traditional *batakari* or smock over a polar-neck sweat shirt. Beside that picture were his name and titles 'Rev. Professor Kwame Bediako, FGA' and accompanied by the words: 'Man of God, Visionary, Inspirer, Builder, Theologian, Scholar, Teacher, Husband and Father who served God and His people in Africa.' These are not exaggerated claims but it is his mentor, Andrew F. Walls, who completes the story by further describing Bediako as 'essentially a world Christian' (Walls 2008:192). This was due to the fact that in all his ministry, networking and scholarship, Bediako consistently said, wrote, and demonstrated that the phenomenal growth in African Christianity should never be misconstrued to mean that the faith had ceased to matter in its former heartlands in the West (Bediako 1995). Thus, although the centre for mission and applied theology, which he founded, revolved around the encounter between Christianity and primal religion in Africa, he also designed and offered courses on world Christian history. That course covered developments within two millennia and on six continents, and even the course on primal religions made room for looking at the primal worldviews of the peoples of Europe and their early interaction with the gospel.

Kwame Bediako, as Walls observes, could have had a successful academic career in Africa or in the West, either in his original discipline of French literature, or in his post-conversion discipline of theology (Funeral Tribute 2008:25). But he resisted attempts to follow convention and, over many years, pointed to Africa's proper place in contemporary worldwide Christian discourse. This culminated in the establishment of a new type of theological institution in Africa where 'devotion to scholarship and understanding of the cultures of Africa would be pursued in a setting of Christian worship, discipleship and mission' (Walls 2008:188). Thus, when in 1996, Kwame Bediako was elected a Fellow of the Ghana Academy of Arts and Sciences, Christian G. Baëta, who sponsored his application, described him as follows:

> *He has applied his considerable expertise as a thinker and a scholar in French literature to his latter found vocation as Pastor and Theologian in his very thorough analysis of the central problem of the African Christian, namely his or her cultural identification with biblical theology. His in-depth studies showed that there was no cultural or philosophical incompatibility between the traditional values of the African and his Christian beliefs and precepts (Funeral Tribute 2008:9).*

Kwame and Mary Gillian met in Bordeaux and they married in 1973. The marriage was blessed with two sons – Nana Yaw Nkansah and Kwabena Dakwa. The couple worked closely together, and Mary Gillian continues to serve as Deputy Rector and Documentation Officer at the Akrofi-Christaller Institute. Following Kwame's dramatic conversion experience, Mary Gillian notes how her husband read through the Bible several times and eventually decided to study theology, beginning at what was then the London Bible College. Here, his academic brilliance became evident as Kwame obtained a first class in theology and proceeded to Ghana to teach for a while at the Christian Service College, Kumasi. During this period, Kwame was accepted into the ordained ministry of the Presbyterian Church of Ghana and then granted permission to continue his theological studies at the University of Aberdeen under the tutelage of Andrew F. Walls. His thesis, which he completed in 1983, was later to be published as *Theology and Identity: The Impact of Culture upon Christian Thought in the Second Century and in Modern Africa* (Oxford: Regnum).

The published version of Kwame Bediako's thesis was nominated as a finalist for the 1993 Harper-Collins Religious Book Award. When the Bediakos returned to Ghana in 1984, he first served as Resident Presbyterian Chaplain of the Accra Ridge Church, an international inter-denominational congregation. He combined this with several other speaking, preaching and teaching engagements. During this tenure at Ridge, Kwame Bediako was also a part-time lecturer in Comparative Religion and African Traditional Religions at the Trinity Theological Seminary, Legon, Accra. His relationship with the seminary continued even after establishing the Akrofi-Christaller Institute. Kwame Bediako was the Guest Speaker at the November 2007 Graduation Ceremony of the Trinity Theological Seminary.

AKROFI-CHRISTALLER INSTITUTE

Kwame Bediako's evangelical faith led him to the 1974 Lausanne Conference on World Evangelization, an encounter that enlarged his world vision and deepened his acquaintance with other Christians from the Two-Thirds World (Walls 2008:189). Kwame and Gillian were at this time already nurturing the vision that led them to eventually establish the Akrofi-Christaller Institute. His acquaintance with other evangelicals from the Two-Thirds World including Vinay Samuel from India, and Rene Padilla, Samuel Escobar and Orlando Costas from Latin America eventually led to the formation of the International Fellowship of Evangelical Mission Theologians (INFEMIT). Subsequently, Kwame formed the related organization, the African Theological Fellowship, as the continental arm of INFEMIT and served as General Secretary under the chairmanship of Bishop David Gitari of Kenya. These were radical evangelical movements of scholars committed to the academic study of Christianity and the validity of its claims against the backdrop of its new contexts in the Third World.

The Akrofi-Christaller Center for Mission, Research and Applied Theology was launched in Accra in November 1986 and finally inaugurated in 1987 at Akropong, the capital of the Akwapim State, in the Eastern Region of Ghana. Johannes Gottlieb Christaller was a 19th century Basel Mission pioneer and Bible translator and Dr. Clement Anderson Akrofi was his 20th century Ghanaian successor. They were both interested in hermeneutics of the mother-tongue. In 1998, the Akrofi-Christaller was granted accreditation as a post-graduate institution offering M.A., M.Th. and Ph.D. programmes in African Christianity in conjunction with the University of Kwazulu-Natal, Pietermaritzburg, South Africa. The University of Kwazulu-Natal appointed Kwame honorary professor in 1998. Hans Visser and Gillian Bediako state the vision of the Akrofi-Christaller Institute as follows:

> *The purpose is to provide training in theology in the African context that equips young scholars to find Christian answers to African questions. This course has the potential for training a new generation of African theologians, and for eventually*

> *attracting students from the West who are open to learn in and from Africa. It is open to both 'evangelicals' and 'ecumenicals', as the aim is to transcend European denominational barriers and the artificial borders between francophone and Anglophone Africa (Visser and Bediako 2000:ix).*

In 2007, Akrofi-Christaller became a fully chartered tertiary institution with a government mandate to award its own degrees. That was when the name of the institution was changed from Akrofi-Christaller Center for Mission, Research and Applied Theology to Akrofi-Christaller Institute for Mission, Theology and Culture. Kwame Bediako gave these initiatives an international character. This was achieved first through his teaching at the Centre for the Study of Christianity in the Non-Western World at the University of Edinburgh; second, through Kwame's committment to other international speaking engagements and third, through programme links developed with other international institutions, such as the Oxford Centre for Mission Studies and the Hendrik Kraemer Institute in the Netherlands.

BEDIAKO AND CHRISTIAN SCHOLARSHIP IN AFRICA

The driving thought behind Kwame Bediako's work was his firm belief that 'the theology that emerges from the cutting edge of the interaction of the Gospel and culture in Africa has universal relevance and far-reaching significance for the global church' (Visser and Bediako 2008:x). In *Theology and Identity*, his first major work, Kwame Bediako compared theological thought and the issue of Christian identity in the context of gospel and culture in the early centuries of the history of the church and in the writings of significant African theologians. From the early church, Bediako examined the works of Justin Martyr and Clement of Alexandria who sought to identify continuities between Greek Socratic philosophical thought and the Christian faith, and Tatian and Tertulian, who saw a radical discontinuity between the two religious cultures. The 20th century African theologians he examined were Bolaji Idowu, John Mbiti, and Vincent Mulago who argued for continuity between primal religiosity and the Christian faith, and Byang Kato who stood for discontinuity. Bediako saw the failure of mission Christianity to seriously engage with primal religions as resulting in the creation of schizophrenic Christians leading to the perception of Christianity as a foreign religion with no certain answers for the questions faced by its indigenous representatives. He argued, therefore, for the creation of a distinctively African Christian identity through a positive apprehension and engagement with primal worldviews which he considered to be the substructure upon which Christianity itself had been built, even in the former heartlands of the faith in the West.

In 1995, Kwame Bediako published *Christianity in Africa,* which was listed by the *International Bulletin of Missionary Research* as one of the most influential books on mission in the late 20th century. The substance of the book originated from the Duff lectures he gave at the Centre for the Study of Christianity in the Non-Western World, New College, at the University of Edinburgh between 1989 and 1992. As Bediako himself notes, the period of teaching at Edinburgh and the presentation of the Duff lectures offered him the opportunity to explore some of the dimensions of the Christian presence in the modern world which struck him as indicating that it might be entering upon a new phase in its history. Among these dimensions, according to Bediako, 'was the realization that the African continent now had a perhaps surprisingly important place in what was being increasingly recognized as a shift in the whole center of gravity of Christianity as a world faith.' The book then proceeds, in chapters of insightful essays, to explore the extent to which this modern shift of the heartlands of the Christian faith from the Northern to the Southern continents has raised new religious and theological issues regarding the understanding of Christianity itself.

In 2000, Kwame Bediako's writings on Jesus Christ and the meaning of the Christ event for Africa, which he had identified as a new major heartland of Christianity, were also published under the title *Jesus of Africa* (Bediako 2000). It was a welcome collection of previously published material now put together in a single volume that enables us to have access to his Christological thought. In this book he explores the meaning of Christ for Africa by noting that the growth in African Christian presence means that at least in some areas, such as those of Christian theology and Christian religious scholarship generally, the continent would not be marginalized. Using the praise and praises of an illiterate Ghanaian local midwife in the opening chapter, Bediako argues forcefully that Christianity in Africa was now a truly African experience. In the received theology of the West, Africans received much that did not touch them at deeper spiritual levels because it did not answer African questions.

Afua Kuma's oral or grassroots theology, he noted, was one that emanated from where the faith lives and must live continually, in the conditions of life of the community of faith, the theology of the living church, reflecting faith in the living Lord as present reality in daily life' (Bediako 2000:9).

Africa's place in Christian history was a primary concern of Bediako's scholarship as it was of two other distinguished African scholars, Kwesi Dickson and Ogbu Kalu, who have died since 2005. Ironically, at the time of his passing, Kwame Bediako was collecting essays that were to be published as a festschrift to honour the memory of Kwesi Dickson, a fellow Ghanaian. Following Kwame Bediako's departure, the initial collection has now been placed in the *Journal of African Christian Thought* (2007), published by the Akrofi-Christaller Institute and edited by Bediako's widow, Mary Gillian, herself an accomplished scholar in Primal Religions and the Bible (2007). At Bediako's funeral, Kalu and I mused briefly on the appropriate manner to immortalize his memory and legacy: possibly a festschrift and an annual series of lectures in honour of Bediako for his contribution to Christian scholarship, and mission research in Africa. Discussions were still ongoing among interested parties when news reached us that Kalu also also been called to glory.

CONCLUSION

Kwame Bediako has left us an impressive legacy in Christian scholarship and helped to redefine Africa's place in the scheme of the God of mission who revealed himself in Christ. His achievements attest to the power of the Holy Spirit in bringing the best out of those who truly encounter God in Christ. In my thinking, Bediako, in most of his articles, set out to develop his theological thought based on a question initially posed by John V. Taylor in his work, *Primal Vision: Christian Presence amid African Religion* as follows:

> *Christ has been presented as the answer to the questions a white man would ask, the solution to the needs that Western man would feel, the Saviour of the world of the European worldview, the object of the adoration and prayer of historic Christendom. But if Christ were to appear as the answer to the questions that Africans are asking, what would he look like? (Taylor 1963:16).*

This question, as Hans Visser and Mary Gillian Bediako rightly note in their introduction to *Jesus in Africa*, was a major concern of Kwame

Bediako's scholarly and pastoral endeavours. His conviction – and it was impossible to listen to Kwame without hearing a variation of this theme – was that 'God speaks into the African context in African idiom, and that it is through hearing in African mother-tongues 'the great things that God has done' (Acts 2:11), that African theology emerges to edify not only the African church but the church world-wide' (Visser and Bediako 2000:vii).

Kwame Bediako's breakthrough into the theological academy was comparatively shorter than most but his legacy, consisting of his thoughts and contributions, is still with us. They are accessible through his writings and the several doctoral dissertations that are being written on him. The opportunity to celebrate his life together with John Stott, arguably two of the most important evangelical minds of the 20th century, brings to mind one of the stanzas of the popular hymn 'now praise we great and famous men'. The stanza in question reads:

Praise we the glorious names we know;
And they whose names have perished
Lost in the haze of long ago
In silent love be cherished.

God buries his workmen but carries on His work and theirs. May Kwame Bediako's legacy live on and continue to challenge us to place our gifts at the feet of the Lord of mission that each of us would play his or her part in the call to bring Christ to the world. Kwame Bediako is gone, but his legacy is still with us.

Bibliography

Bediako, Kwame (1992, 1999) *Theology and Identity: The Impact of Culture on Christian Thought in the Second Century and Modern Africa.* Oxford: Regnum Books.

Bediako, Kwame (1995) *Christianity in Africa: The Renewal of a Non-Western Religion.* Maryknoll, N.Y.: Orbis Books; Edinburgh: University of Edinburgh.

Bediako, Kwame (1995)'The Significance of Modern African Christianity: a Manifesto. ' *Studies in World Christianity.* 1.1: 51-67.

Bediako, Kwame (2000) *Jesus in Africa: The Christian Gospel in African History and Experience.* Akropong-Akwapim/Yaoundé: Regnum Africa/Editions Clé.

Ekem, John D.K. (2005) *New Testament Concepts in an African Pluralistic Setting.* Accra: Sonlife Press.

Ferdinando, Keith (2007) 'Christian Identity in the African Context: Reflections on Kwame Bediako's Theology and Identity. '*Journal of Evangelical Theological Society.* 50.1:121-143.

Funeral Brochure *Call to Glory: Rev. Professor Manasseh Kwame Bediako.* (July 6, 2008).

Journal of African Christian Thought (In Honor of Kwesi A. Dickson). December 2007, 10, 2.

Visser, Hans and Gillian Bediako (2000) 'Introduction' to Kwame Bediako, *Jesus in Africa: The Christian Gospel in African History and Experience.* Akropong-Akwapim/Yaoundé: Regnum Africa/Editions Clé, vii-xii.

Walls, Andrew F. October (2008) 'Kwame Bediako and Christian Scholarship in Africa.' *International Bulletin of Missionary Research,* vol. 32, 4:188-193.

Taylor, John V. (1963) *Primal Vision: Christian Presence amid African Religion.* London: SCM Press.

DAVID GITARI
CONTRIBUTING TO THE TRANSFORMATION OF POLITICS IN KENYA

REGINALD NALUGALA

Reginald Nalugala is a Kenyan scholar completing his Ph.D. study at OCMS, looking at poverty and development in Kenya. He lectures in governance and development, while co-ordinating a spiritual support programme for Members of Parliament in Nairobi, Kenya.

INTRODUCTION

Archbishop David Gitari has been a great inspiration to most Kenyans and to me personally because of his positive contribution to the transformation of politics in Kenya. I had the privilege of interviewing Archbishop Gitari at his home in Embu on May 12th, 2012. This paper sets out to uncover the world in which he lived and why it was important for him to become the crusader for a democratic society in Kenya. I show why David Gitari epitomizes what it means to be a church leader fighting for social justice in society without mixing too much in local politics. He calls it 'keeping a critical distance', and this defines his approach to transformative politics in Kenya. The background explains the influence of his formative days on his future prophetic ministry, while the methodology that he meticulously and courageously employed to deliver his message during those turbulent days has helped other church leaders to replicate the same in their quest for a just society. The paper concludes with lessons learned from his mission in the local community.

BACKGROUND

Archbishop David Gitari was the third African archbishop and bishop of the diocese of Nairobi in the Anglican Church of Kenya. He was born on September 16, 1937. He attended the famous Kangaru High School in Embu before attending the University of Nairobi for a Bachelor of Arts degree. He married Grace Wanjiru on March 31, 1966 and God blessed them with three children.

He was ordained into the priesthood of the Anglican Church in 1972 by Bishop Obadiah Kariuki. On July 20, 1975, at the age of thirty-seven, Gitari was consecrated and enthroned as the first bishop of Mt. Kenya East diocese. In that position, Gitari founded St. Andrews College of Theology and Development at Kabare. He served there as bishop until 1990 when Mt. Kenya East diocese was split into Embu and Kirinyaga dioceses. He then moved to Kirinyaga, becoming the first bishop of Kirinyaga. During his tenure as bishop of Mount Kenya East (1975-90) and of Kirinyaga (1990-96), there was phenomenal church growth in these two dioceses. As evangelism was his first priority, he led many missions in African universities. These initiatives were creatively combined with development, theological education, liturgical renewal, and the encouragement of women's ordination. He served for many years as chairman of the provincial board of theological education in the Anglican Church of Kenya. He served four times as chair of the National Council of Churches of Kenya and acted as a mediator between the international evangelical and ecumenical movements. He also served as chairman of the board of St. Paul's United Theological College, Limuru. He was a member of the Anglican Roman Catholic International Commission (from 1983-1990). David Gitari became the Anglican Archbishop of Kenya from 1997 -2002. He was a founding member of the Oxford Centre for Mission Studies (OCMS) in 1983. He continued to sit on the OCMS board until 2003. Bishop Gitari has been called many names: Dr. Ben Knighton refers to him as a modern prophet to the Kenyan nation, the lens through which one can examine the role of the church in determining the politics of a young nation while at the same time capturing the contrasting political initiatives and responses by Christian leaders. Gitari has written and edited many books and articles including *In Season and Out of Season: Sermons to a Nation* (1996) and *Let the Bishop Speak* (1988). In his consecration speech on September 22, 2002, Benjamin Nzimbi, fourth Kenyan African archbishop and bishop of All Saints diocese, paid tribute to his predecessor, Dr. David Gitari, for his bold leadership. The newly consecrated Archbishop Nzimbi also quoted a Kiswahili poem praising Dr. Gitari: '*Gitari ni hodari. Gitari ni daktari. Gitari ni jemedari. Gitari ni hatari.*' (Gitari is bold. Gitari is a doctor. Gitari is an army commander. Gitari is dangerous). Nzimbi vowed to emulate him by walking in his footsteps.

On July 14, 1998, Gitari was made an honorary Doctor of Divinity by the University of Kent. He retired on September 16, 2002 as archbishop of the Anglican Church of Kenya. He will be remembered for his bold messages on social justice in Kenya from the pulpit. Along with fellow clergymen such as Reverend Njoya, Bishop Okullu, and Bishop Muge, Gitari had the courage to criticize and hold the government accountable for its actions. Like Muge, Gitari believed in the power of the pulpit to transform and reform society. Using the power of the spoken word, Gitari scared politicians by pointing to their wrongly acquired wealth, and the fact that they were enriching themselves at the expense of the poor.

When I interviewed Archbishop Gitari one could not believe that he was now retired from mainstream church administration work. His daily routine had not changed much. His phone kept on ringing and from the answers he gave, you knew this was a politician, or State House, or this was the head teacher of a school who needed wise counsel on teenage delinquency. He believes that God's worker never retires even when the body requires panel-beating to make it straight. He continues to fight to uphold and defend human rights. He was a member of the Constitution of Kenya Review Commission (CKRC) and fully participates in the constitutional review process as one of the representatives of Kenyan faith-based organizations. He also travels, preaches, and gives presentations, calling upon Christians to embrace a culture of peace-making and conflict resolution.

In March 2012, he was involved in a controversy when he supported a youth movement which was opposed to select leadership in central Kenya. It was brutally dispersed so incensing Gitari. The rally was eventually allowed on 30th May 2012 attended by Gitari. The moderate Kenya News Agency of 31st May 2012 reported that the chief guest, retired Archbishop David Gitari gave the keynote speech urging Kenyans to approach the next elections as nationalists not tribalists. Quoting the Constitution and the Political Parties Act, he condemned parties that were not national in outlook.

Gitari is an example of a modern prophet who does not fear to brush the rattlesnake of Kenyan politics. Thanks to his persistent crusades for social justice from 1978, Kenyans can now enjoy a new constitution that offers more freedom. But what influenced Gitari's ministry and the methods employed to deliver his prophetic ministry? Gitari said that

Josiah Mwangi Kariuki, known as JM, and then Member of Parliament for Nyandarua North, inspired him through his commitment to social justice in the newly independent Kenya. Gitari's known prophetic ministry began early in 1975 after the assassination of this populist and flamboyant Kenyan politician. Blamuel Njururi, 1975 Journalist of the Year Award Winner, says of him: 'J. M. was not an ordinary Member of Parliament, but a visionary, who was one of the best socio-politically focused leaders at the time of his death.' Gitari took upon himself to criticize the government for the deaths of other key politicians but also warned against those taking tribal oaths as a result of the assassination of JM to kill their neighbours:

> *An appeal for national unity must be an appeal that may be united in truth, but not in falsehood. It is quite possible for a tribe or group of people to unite by entering into a secret superstitious oath. That kind of unity is founded on fear, not truth...Once a person is set free from bondage of superstition; he is freed from secret tribal oaths'.*[1]

As a Christian student leader at the University of Nairobi in 1988, I invited the bishop to respond to an earlier sermon on the theme: 'United we stand, divided we fall'. When he came to speak to us many things were not going right in Kenya. However, his pastoral work led him into political controversy. He preached and campaigned against land-grabbing by powerful politicians; he challenged economic injustice on a national as well as a local level. He preached against constitutional changes which introduced voting by queuing (in a specific place, publicly indicating your chosen candidate) instead of by secret ballot. He noticed that the person with the shortest queue won and the one with the numerical majority lining up behind him ended up losing. When he criticized the Mlolongo voting system, the Kenya Government, under President Moi, thought of him as a rebel-rouser. The ruling party leaders angrily responded that a man of the cloth should not concentrate on preaching politics from the pulpit. From 1980, Gitari became a symbol of hope to the voiceless people of Kenya at a time when the country needed to reform the way it conducted its style of governance in the management of national resources. Indeed, one cannot speak of church and politics in Kenya without bringing the name of Archbishop Gitari into the discussion.

Church Leaders and Politics

A question raised by David Gitari was whether politics should be left to politicians and faith matters to church leaders. As I discussed this with Gitari, we considered many situations that require cross-fertilization from both sides. There were religious leaders who had crossed over to politics by being elected Members of Parliament e.g. Rev. Mutava Musyimi, Bishop Wanjiru of a Pentecostal Church in Nairobi. Gitari lamented Rev. Musyimi's decision: he felt that his position was stronger while in office as secretary general of the umbrella body of the churches of Kenya, and that the moment he crossed over to politics his influence waned. Nobody would trust him anymore, and the voice of the church was silenced. The person whom people had trusted as their spokesman had abandoned them. Gitari felt that to be relevant, a critical distance should be maintained between politics and the church, and yet religion and politics should work hand in hand. Where this has not happened there has been more corruption and injustice in society. Gitari has followed in the footsteps of other Kenyan bishops to justify why the clergy can speak about politics.

Gitari's deep concern for the Kenyan people was not without cost. On the night of April 21, 1989, at the height of his struggle for justice, a large and heavily armed gang of thugs numbering about 100 raided his house. They dug out the security bars and shouted that they had come to kill him. He and his family escaped to the roof and called for help from neighbours who came to his rescue just in time and the thugs fled. Over 38,000 faithful well-wishers attended a service in and outside an unattractive building in Kerugoya to give thanks for the deliverance of their bishop from political thuggery.

Gitari moved from being a strict separationist who insisted that there should be a wall between faith and politics to a direct interventionist who agreed that religious communities should participate as organized interest groups in all phases of elective and legislative politics. How did this happen?

This journey started for him with the Lausanne Conference in 1974. He had come from the Revival Movement which had not been involved in critiquing the politics of the day. The East African Revival Movement was born in Rwanda in the early 1930s and spread to Burundi, Kenya, Tanzania, and Uganda. The East African Revival is still on-going, and has been a great stimulus to the church but it tended to be inward-looking rather than outward-looking. Whenever the revivalists meet, the first thing they do is share a testimony. What does God mean to you since we last met? What sins have you committed which you can confess and then we can pray for you? Involvement in politics was anathema and they would say very clearly that a Christian brother who turns to politics was a lukewarm brother. To them, politics was a dirty game.

When Gitari went to the Lausanne Congress on World Evangelization in 1974, he discovered arguments from John Stott and others that 'evangelicals should confess to having put a wedge between evangelism and socio-political action'. Gitari returned to Kenya, holding that as one of the biggest challenges. He recognized that in order to transform the world one cannot avoid socio-political action. Through the International Fellowship of Mission Theologians (INFEMIT), like-minded theologians such as Gitari have continued to meet. They challenged one another on the whole issue of faith and politics.

Gitari said that as a Christian leader he learned a great deal from the story of Jethro in Exodus chapter 18, in terms of understanding his priorities. Firstly, you must be the people's representative before God and bring their disputes to him. Secondly, teach them and show them the way to live. Thirdly, select people who can help with the work. He felt that women as well as have roles to play in the ministry of God.

In 1997, when the church leaders were trying to fight to change the constitution to allow it to become more democratic before the elections in December, Gitari led a delegation of church leaders to see President Moi and gave him a memorandum of 15 pages to protest the many injustices his government was committing to the people of Kenya. The opposition leaders used to meet at Ufungamano House (an Ecumenical Centre next to the University of Nairobi) and at times would meet at the All Saints Cathedral in Nairobi, to protest against Moi's autocratic rule. In most cases, the police would be sent to beat them, even following them into the cathedral with tear gas. They were beaten and bleeding inside the cathedral. That day was shown on world television when Gitari cleansed the cathedral by spraying holy water everywhere and then preached to them from Daniel chapter five. The following Tuesday, the president invited him to State House and told him, 'I now agree you can change the constitution before the elections'. This was the beginning of the drafting of a new constitution for Kenya which was unveiled on 27th August 2010 witnessed by world leaders and Kenyans.

Meeting John Stott

David Gitari first met John Stott at the University of Nairobi (1961). Gitari was the chairman of the Christian Union at the University. They became very close friends from that moment onwards. Archbishop Gitari recalls two incidents that made him know John Stott better. The first was in 1961, when John Stott came as their chief guest during the Revival Spirit Conference at the University. Over 300 students registered and faithfully attended all the sessions each day for a week. On the closing day of the conference, John Stott went to the microphone to ask those who had been moved by the spirit of the Lord to come forward and be blessed. Only one man out of the 300 present came forward. This man was called Ephraim Githinji.

He is still alive and in contact with David Gitari. He retired from active public life. John Stott was not just very disappointed but also asked himself whether the gospel of Christ could find root in Africa at this rate. That was the first time David says he saw John Stott so angry. For John Stott, David explained, salvation was supposed to be instant. The first experience on triggered a silent meditation in Gitari's heart on how to deal with multitudes when you know they are seeking things deeper than the spirit. John Stott became a frequent visitor of Gitari in Kenya. The second experience was when Gitari discovered that John Stott loved birds and being on the lake. Whenever John would visit Gitari they would go to Lake Naivasha and hire a boat. John would spend hours and hours admiring the birds through his binoculars. Gitari was always bored but he chuckled about this. In order to behave like an endearing good African, he accompanied John but carried all the newspapers like the Weekly Review, the church magazine called Target (produced since 1957) and more theological books to read and write his sermons. John would ask Gitari if he saw the big malibu, the kite, or the eagle catch a fish. Gitari would nod as if he did see but continued to read his notes.

His Encounter with Kwame Bediako

Gitari met Kwame Bediako at Lausanne in 1974. They became close friends working together on the OCMS board and on promoting the ideals of

INFEMIT. They travelled together to Bangkok and Mexico. They were founding members of the Africa Theological Fraternity (ATF). He described Kwame as a man of tremendous energy, intelligence and a great scholar. Kwame had two Ph.D.s, one in French and the other in English. That source of knowledge was a great resource to INFEMIT and Gitari as a person because when it came to writing good conference papers, Kwame would contribute the final paper. He was shaken when Kwame passed away in June 2008. You could not talk of Kwame without mentioning how close Chris Sugden, Vinay Samuel, and Rene Padilla were to David Gitari: men of great vision and energy who continue today to contribute to modern evangelism.

Promoting Peace in Kenya and within the Church

As archbishop, Gitari worked to restore peace and unity in the church and to resolve the many divisions and quarrels in various dioceses. Many dioceses had no bishops due to accusations of tribalism and nepotism during elections and appointments of bishops and clergy. Gitari also revived training institutions, especially the Anglican Theological Education by Extension (TEE) programme, which was floundering in many dioceses. With the help of grants from Trinity Church, New York, he helped to set up the Anglican website so that all dioceses could have access to internet services, making communication and networking easier.

There were family challenges. His younger brother passed away very early in his married life. Gitari had to take the responsibility for bringing up the deceased brother's children as his own which was not always easy.

Lessons We Can Learn from Gitari's Experiences

Gitari used different analogies to describe some of his ideas. In one factory, the management discovered that there were many accidents. They decided to buy ambulances to take the injured to hospital. For them this was the social action they could offer to their own. However, they did not want to ask why there were so many accidents. The moment they asked that question they discovered that the work place was congested, machines were old and outdated and safety rules were not observed. When new machines were bought and the place expanded, the number of accidents was almost zero. There was no need to have an ambulance crew. Gitari argued that what the management was doing in handling the welfare of the workers was what he called social work without social action. This is what the politicians do when church leaders want to correct social ills. They are told to buy ambulances and not to ask why there are so many accidents.

The second example is that politics cannot be left to politicians alone, unless we all want to sink. Gitari gave an analogy of a man who took his friend fishing in a hired boat. When they reached the middle of the lake, the friend started sawing the boat into two instead of fishing as his friend did. The man cutting the boat into two was asked what he was doing. Did he want to drown? The friend answered that he should mind his own business. There was an argument and they agreed to co-operate and save the boat. Therefore, for Gitari ministry is not just to save souls but to preach a holistic reconciliatory gospel. Matthew 9:26 has been important for his ministry. It is where Jesus went to every city and synagogue preaching the good news. He saw many people haggard and harassed, disillusioned and hungry. He decided to appoint the twelve to help him in preaching the holistic gospel that the people were looking for.

Teilhard de Chardin, used to say in reference to the power of withdrawal, that 'Nothing can go on if we leave the table, neither can any power force us to remain...fight within and not without'. Gitari attended the Lambeth Conference in 1998. This was at the height of emerging controversies about ordaining women priests and gay marriage. His spoke against gay marriage but he did not believe in the question of the split of church because transformation should take place inside the church rather than when the church is split.

David Gitari has followed the doctrine of Aikido, which is the power of flexibility to emerging changes, an art that practitioners could use to defend themselves while also protecting their attacker from injury. Gitari believes that the process of transformation is not going on a long journey and when you arrive there you say my job is done. He believes it is a continuous spiral circle with new landmarks at every turn of your travel which require scholarship, research and interpretation in the right context. Tolstoy summed up well what Archbishop David Gitari has come to criticize,' I sit on a man's back, choking him and making him carry me, and yet assure myself and others that I am very sorry for him and wish to lighten his load by all possible means- except by getting off his back'. Gitari continues to remind the political establishment in Kenya that they must get off the back of Kenyans who continue to carry heavy burdens economically, politically, socially and spiritually. Therefore, scholarship demands we cannot step in the same water twice as Heraclitus once observed. The church speaks for both the poor and the elite of society. Positions change very quickly and we must be aware of that. The financial crisis of 2008 has taught us many lessons as those who were once rich lost most of their savings reducing them to paupers. Some are now leading lives which they never imagined they would.

CONCLUSION

Gitari was involved in the democratic and political process but he also learnt to keep a critical distance. As a bishop, he saw the practice of a holistic gospel as essential if there is to be change in developing countries. Three priorities stood out: evangelism, teaching ministry and social justice. Under social justice, his priorities were water, agriculture (food), improving parishes and seeking self-reliance, and education. The government approved when churches built schools, hospitals, and colleges but when the church leaders asked why there were so many accidents, poor leadership, or why certain parts of Kenya had no food when others are throwing food away, the political establishment called that interfering in politics.

Even though Gitari was an Anglican clergyman, he walked the path of ecumenism. It was through ecumenism that he was a priest in the Presbyterian Church and the Baptist Church from 1972. He continues to warn against 'religious tribalism' emerging in the Christian churches. To him, every denomination symbolises a certain spirituality that helps their followers grow in the gospel of Christ rather than making the denominations themselves the gospel.

He is against violence and revolutions which shed blood. He says that transformational leaders never say 'Amen' and fade away but continue to rediscover themselves in new situations each day. Because they have the framework of interrogating that emerging change they can continue to be relevant. Gitari and his friends continue to see the agenda for mission in the Global South and the whole world.

He does not harbour any regrets in his life. He lives by the same zeal he had when he was appointed bishop. At 74 years old, he keeps himself in prayer and research. His legs are beginning to let him down, but his mind remains active and he himself hovers between his Philadelphia home and the political landscape of Kenya.

BIBLIOGRAPHY

Bediako, K. (1999) *Theology and identity: Impact of Culture on Christianity thought in the second Century in Modern Africa.* Oxford: Regnum International.

Benson, G. Patrick (1995) 'Ideological Politics versus Biblical Politics: Kenya's Protestant churches and the Nyayo Churches' in Hansen and Twaddle (1995), pp. 177-99.

Gitari, David M. and Benson, G.P. (eds.) (1986) Witnessing to the Living God in contemporary Africa : findings and papers of the inaugural meeting of Africa Theological Fraternity. Nairobi: ATF.

Haugerud, Angelique (1995) *The Culture of Politics in Modern Kenya.* Cambridge: Cambridge University Press.

Karanja, John K. (1999) *Founding an African Faith: Kikuyu Anglican Christianity, 1900-1945.* Nairobi: Uzima Press.

Knighton, B. (2009) (ed.) *Religion and Politics in Kenya: Essays in Honour of a Meddlesome Priest.* Basingstoke: Palgrave Macmillan.

Catharine Feser Padilla
Bible, Bed and Bread: A Matter of Distance

Ruth Padilla DeBorst

Ruth Padilla DeBorst, a resident of Costa Rica, serves as Director of Christian Formation and Leadership Development with World Vision International, as Coordinator of the Networking Team of The International Fellowship for Mission as Transformation (INFEMIT) and as board member of the Latin American Theological Fellowship (FTL).

'Caty me enseñó dos cosas (Cathy taught me two things),' shared Roberto at the crowded memorial service. 'She taught me to respect women and to eat bean sprouts!' Thanks to her striking blend of tenacious faith, servant love, conviction and common sense, the teaching and modeling impact of 'Caty' -as she is known in Latin America- ranged broadly: from hermeneutics to nutritious budget cooking, from parenting priorities to New Testament Greek and Bible Study methods, from piano playing to lecturing and publishing. From Argentina to Mexico her influence was felt.

However, Caty was not originally from Latin America. How, then, did she end up spending most of her life in that part of the world, what did she do there, and what was the key to her involvement in God's work of transformation for fifty years in lands so far from the ones in which her life had begun? After painting a portrait of Catharine and her contributions to God's mission in Latin America, I here propose that it is all a matter of distance. Catharine's ministry is still fruitful beyond her death because, just as the Lord she served, she did not remain aloof, comfortable in the security of the world she knew; instead she drew near, opening her very heart and home to welcome and affirm, to awaken and equip, women and men, and particularly those most in need. She not only moved to Latin America. She allowed God to move Latin America into her heart.

Marrying Latin America

A grand-daughter of Swiss-German and Scotch-Irish immigrants, Caty was born in Philadelphia on November 5, 1932. She lost her mother when she was six years old, and grew up with her single dad and sister in Coatsville, PA, until she went off to Wheaton College, where she earned her Bachelors of Arts degree in 1954. Between undergraduate and graduate school, she served as a chaplain at Slaten Farms, a girls' reformatory, with the warm support of members of the Blue Church, of Springfield, PA. She returned to Wheaton for her M.A. in New Testament, and it was there, in the International Mission Fellowship, that Cathy began stepping across cultural and linguistic barriers. Moreover, her eyes focused more on Latin America when she began driving an Ecuadorean fellow-student every Sunday to a small church of Latin American immigrants. Upon graduation she moved to Nebraska to serve InterVarsity in the region of Nebraska and South Dakota.

Cathy's commitment to service in Latin America was clinched when she agreed to marry an old Ecuadorean friend, Rene Padilla, who had returned to Latin America and was serving with the International Fellowship of Evangelical Students (IFES). With their wedding in 1961, she bought a one-way ticket to Latin America and never turned back.

Her first-hand, cross-cultural journey began in Colombia and continued through Ecuador, England, and Peru before its longest chapter, in Buenos Aires, Argentina, where the youngest two of the couple's five children were born. While most missionaries lived in exclusive neighbourhoods, close to private schools and to other expatriates, Caty's choice was to settle into a regular, working-middle-class area, and to send her kids into the neighbourhood public school. So, though products of an Ecuadorean Dad and a US born Mom, the kids grew up as run-of-the-mill Argentines.

The partnership with her husband of nearly 49 years took on many shapes: packing and airport-shuttling for his many trips; proof-reading and commenting on the papers he presented in world forums; wrangling with him over the translation of Greek biblical terms; weathering the constant threat of a military dictatorship bent on exterminating anyone they considered radical; making ends meet during times of economic limitation; sharing the parenting of their children and ministry in and through their local church, Iglesia Evangélica Bautista de La Lucila, the International Fellowship of Evangelical Students, the Latin American Theological Fellowship, the Kairos Foundation, and the Latin America Mission.

A Mother, Teacher and Model

Caty's parenting extended far beyond her biological children and her humble hospitality reached far beyond politely receiving an occasional overnight guest. The poor, needy, and vulnerable were not a class for her; they were not cases out there to be considered at arms' length. They were real people with first and last names, with gifts and stories, needs and dreams. Outside the home, and with unflinching stamina, Caty lugged food to stock church day-care centres for deprived children; she read for hours to blind students; she risked being mugged or beaten, in order to accompany slum dwellers and drug addicts in their neighbourhoods. Furthermore, she opened her heart and home, patiently offering bread and bed, counsel and comfort to those in need, often for months at a time: like several teenagers with trouble at home; like the single mom, needing care for her toddler while she worked and studied to get ahead in life; like the family of a recovering drug addict – mom, dad and three children-- whom Caty welcomed into her already full home for several months. In addition, unforgettable to all who attended were yearly Christmas dinners: around Caty's table gathered the most unlikely juxtaposition of people! The young man just out of jail, the recently immigrated Czechoslovakian family, the schizophrenic Polish woman, they all joined in an appropriate celebration of the God who became a poor refugee baby in a remote corner of the Roman Empire.

Beyond the home front, as an acute New Testament scholar and teacher of Greek, hermeneutics and Bible study methods, Caty also influenced generations of students and pastors at the Instituto Bíblico Buenos Aires and the Seminario Evangélico Interdenominacional in San Fernando. Students to her were not simply minds ready to be filled with concepts. They were real people wanting to be encouraged as whole-life disciples of Jesus Christ. So, she could just as well insist on a meticulous translation of some New Testament text as entertain a baby so her father could write his exam. At the same time, her teaching was not restricted to formal settings: she led Bible studies, especially for women, at home and at church as well as in several local slums and in student conferences across the continent. As a co-founder of the Kairos Foundation, she not only became the longest-standing board member (1989-2009), but she also contributed to most of Kairos' programmes. Meanwhile, behind the scenes, she offered endless chauffeur services and an ever-listening ear and quiet wise counsel to team members, from kitchen staff to page designers, from programme directors to fellow board members.

Through the handbook that she authored, *La Palabra de Dios para el Pueblo de Dios* (God's Word for God's People, Ediciones Kairos, 2007), her Bible teaching ministry continues reaching deep and wide. So do her other publications, which focus mainly on the role of women and men as equal bearers of God's image in the kingdom of God, the church and the world. This role she confidently modeled and inspired in her own children and in generations of Latin American women and men. As a woman, and undaunted by the prevailing *machista* culture around her, she opened the way for women continent-wide to integrate their multiple vocations, as single women, as wives, as professionals – theologians, teachers, writers, preachers, and many more – as full citizens, alongside men, as God's people, and as active agents in search of God's kingdom and God's justice.

One of her most abiding legacies is the Center of Interdisciplinary Theological Studies (CETI). A strong team of Bible scholars, theologians, psychologists, educators, philosophers and medical professionals designed the curriculum that is organized around the four main areas of Church, Family, Work and Society. The programme was originally produced for university graduates seeking to strengthen their theological perspective as they engaged in their diverse professions. Caty not only served as Dean of the Center but also oversaw the adaptation of the material for a simpler, diploma level programme more accessible to pastors and lay leaders. She coached and encouraged women and men from across around Latin America as they grappled with building connections between God's Word and God's world. Today, the material is being used within Latin America and around the world. More importantly, hundreds of church leaders have stepped out in daring expressions of mission, among disaffected teenagers and gang members, in prophetic denunciation of injustice, in re-casting their marriages and partnerships, thanks to the work of God through this programme to which Caty gave so much.

CATY AND JOHN STOTT

The only years Cathy and her family lived outside Latin America were the ones they spent in Manchester, while her husband, René Padilla, worked on his Ph.D. During those years, 1963-1965, the couple visited John Stott in his modest apartment at 12 Weymouth Street in London.

A closer relationship with 'Uncle John' grew during his four visits to Argentina. The first two were in February of 1974 and July of 1977, in connection with pastoral forums and the obligatory bird-watching opportunities. In February 1980, John joined the entire Padilla family on a camping vacation in Patagonia. It became very obvious those days of sleeping on the ground with tents battered by the wind, that both John and Cathy shared and inspired in others the values of simplicity, austerity and appreciation for the small beauties of life in addition to their love for the Word of God and their passion to connect that Word to the world they lived in.

In 2001, during this last visit to Argentina, along with Chris Wright, the family and the Kairos community celebrated John's 80th birthday. And finally, in September of 2008, Cathy and Rene visited their old friend John at his last earthly home, St. Barnabas College, Lingfield. Little did any of the three imagine that he would outlive her by almost two years, although he was nine years her senior.

Incarnation as the Paradigm for Mission: A Matter of Distance

Caty's incarnation in Latin America was so thorough that, although she was officially classed as a 'missionary', supported with her husband by the offerings of churches and personal donors channeled through IFES and later the Latin America Mission, the expected barriers of culture and language were far superseded by the love she shared. She became not only an insider but a mother to many. 'She was a reflection of Jesus Christ among us,' reminisces a pastor. 'Her figure was small but it turned big in service to others. As for Jesus, her priority always was other people', recalls one woman. Another echoes, 'In becoming a mother to me she taught me to be a mother.' And one of her students affirms, 'She taught us that people are more important than anything. She taught us to love and respect Scripture. She taught us to live!'

In sum, Catharine's legacy is that of a woman so taken by the amazing truth of God's love, of *God with us*, that she daily followed Jesus as a faithful disciple and put her exceptional Spirit-given gifts to the humble service of others, especially the most vulnerable people around her, not from a distance, but engaging alongside them. She did so in lands far from her birthplace, in cultures other than her original one, and in a language she only learned as an adult. I never asked her, but I can only imagine that, by God's grace, when she drew close to women and men, younger and older, like Dominga and Adriana, Laura and Moira, Tati and Alicia, Quique and Roberto, she recognized Christ in their faces. That, I propose, was the key that allowed her to treat people with respect, even when others and they themselves saw nothing worthy in it. When she saw Christ in them, it came naturally: she glimpsed people's strengths and potential, their gifts and capacities where others and they themselves saw only failure and insurmountable difficulties. By drawing near them, loving and adopting them unconditionally into her circle of equals, of care and counsel, of respect for women and bean sprouts, she enlisted them as worthy, beautiful members of God's people, as women and men, families and communities able to actively contribute to God's good purposes in God's good world.

And as Caty incarnated in Latin soil, she too was transformed. Although ever true to her tough and self-sufficient Northern European stock, through making her home in Latin America, she was stretched into an ever more sensitive, warm and caring US-Latin American. Her identification with the people moulded her to such an extent that when her husband was offered attractive opportunities to teach in the United States, and to move with the family, all expenses paid, she insisted that they turn the offers down because, in her own words, 'Argentina is home and this is where we belong.'

Although, until the end, her pronunciation gave away her non-Latin origin, few editors achieved such mastery of the Spanish language as Caty. And, although she never learned to enjoy '*mate*' tea, the staple drink of Argentines, by making her home in Buenos Aires and opening it up so freely, Caty made known to others the God who does not watch us from a distance but who has drawn ever so near; the God-community who walks with us and yearns to live in community with us. The God-community who invites us to dine, work, love, build, study, serve, live the whole of our lives, close up, exposed, open to God's love and moved by it to love others. There is no greater mission than making that love visible, as Caty did, through the Bible, bed and bread. It is all a matter of distance.

JUAN JOSÉ BARREDA WALKING IN THE STEPS OF JESUS

MARCELO VARGAS

Marcelo Vargas is a Bolivian mission practitioner working among indigenous Andean people. He also serves as Executive Secretary of Latin American Theological Fraternity.

WAY IN

There are many ways of walking in the steps of Jesus. We do it when his image is built holistically into our lives and ministries through the power of the Holy Spirit. Another way is when we obediently mould our lives into His teaching, in a lifestyle of radical followers of Christ. The third way is the combination of both, the work of God in us and the personal willingness of having Christ as our Lord. The socio-history of Juan José Barreda is a contemporary Latin American experience of walking in the footsteps of Jesus as an individual and as a servant to others.

BIOGRAPHY

Juan José Barreda was born in a Christian Catholic home, in Peru in 1967. His father was a known union leader who later actively participated in the Peruvian Agrarian Reform. His mother was a housewife who cared for her four children. From a young age, Juan José breathed the atmosphere of community work and active participation in society. In their community, his father organized peasant co-operatives and gave them advice on organization. Sometimes he spent weeks in the countryside and, upon his return, he used to share his experiences with the family. Juan José (JJ) had many opportunities to travel with his father and see the socio-political conditions.

Despite living in the city, JJ lived in an environment closely related to the countryside and to popular education. It was only in his adolescence and youth that he began to realize that most educational places and churches were not participating in community matters. JJ sewed shirts, made tables, sowed seeds in fields, so learning many aspects of the reality of his society.

His parents were committed Catholics and this also marked JJ's life. Masses were held on Sunday night on the edge of a hill close to their home, as there was no church. Several friends would come to prepare the place for the mass. They used to take buckets of water to settle the soil so that there would not be too much dust, while another person brought a small table from his home to use as an altar. The priest arrived always a couple of hours early, having got off the van that left him at the corner. He was always dressed in faded blue jeans, sandals and a white shirt. After arranging the place before the Mass, he used the water from one of the buckets and washed his face and hands. He dried himself and put on the white robe with a coloured belt, Inca style, around his waist. The reading of the Bible was communal. A person would come forward and share a personal life situation. Somebody else would suggest a biblical passage that referred to it and they talked about it. There were about 60 people illuminated by a few lamps. Some neighbours also organized Bible studies with study guides. They used the 'God speaks today' Bible translation. JJ's sister was part of the group that played guitars at the Mass and he soon learned to play as well. At that time, when university students were fighting for human rights, their prayer requests were for justice and for their safety during the military retaliations against them. JJ remembered that his brother was taken to jail for participating in a demonstration with other boys of the parish youth movement. 'El Chino', the priest, visited JJ's family while his dad tried to find out in which police station his brother was being held. Praying for prisoners, visiting neighbours' homes, thinking about faith in political terms, praying and studying the Scriptures in community – this was JJ's church life when he was young.

It was not until he was finishing high school that some friends invited JJ to an evangelical church. He did not like the idea of going and when he mentioned it at home the reactions were quite negative. But there was a small gathering of young people and his best friends were going, so he participated in the meeting because it was a Bible study environment celebrating God's work and brotherhood. They were intrigued that he knew so much about the Bible. It was a participatory environment, where his opinions were taken into account and he felt he could share his thoughts with others about what he was experiencing as a person and what they were experiencing as a country. JJ remembered they spoke about having Christ as their Lord and Saviour and he told them that he already had Him, but he prayed as they suggested and followed Jesus more closely. At first, there were many fights with his parents about this decision to join the evangelical church. His father was very nationalistic and linked Protestantism with foreigners. However, they decided to give him the freedom to choose. His parents made a gesture he still remembers. One morning, on his 17th birthday, his dad gave him a black book with a leather cover. When JJ saw it, he realized it was a Reina Valera version of the Bible. They were not allowed to take the 'God speaks today' Bible to the evangelical church. That gift was significant. He has that Bible with him as a remembrance of love, ecumenism and respect.

WALKING IN HIS STEPS IN DISCIPLESHIP

Jesus enables us to walk in his footsteps when his image is built holistically in our lives and ministries through the power of the Holy Spirit.

At the age of 18, JJ felt a call from God for ministry. He was starting his studies in systems engineering at the university and he decided to talk to his parents about studying theology at the Baptist Bible Seminary in Lima. His parents gave him permission to study theology on the condition that he would not stop studying at the university. Again, it was a great show of respect to his faith because, even as practicing Catholics, they paid for all the studies at the evangelical Seminary. The church and the seminary were fundamentalist and their vision of community practices appeared similar to those he had experienced.

The home group meetings affected JJ. There he experienced the communion of bible study among friends, with contemporary questions and challenging approaches. But there was a particular meeting in the 'Caserio' that made a lasting impression on him. The 'Caserio' were the homes of the peasant farmers and ranchers about two miles from the church. The very poor little houses were constructions made out of wood, cane and zinc. The people who lived there were mostly African Latinos and indigenous people. They used to arrive walking in the afternoons when the sun was setting. The cookers used coal, while candles and lamps were the lights. Drinking water came from a tanker truck that came every day and deposited water in barrels or plastic buckets. He and his friend were very young but they were treated as special guests. JJ realized no one ever visited them and they lived marginalized from the rest of society. They started going there because one of the brothers was evangelical and had begun to go to JJ's church. Once, in a conversation, this brother in Christ shared that there were people who were interested in hearing from God but did not want to come to church. JJ remembered how poor his clothes were and the mud stains on his shoes. JJ and his friend started by asking them about their lives. For JJ, it was a crisis to hear their life stories. To discover a world he had only seen, but now, with them as brothers and friends, he also began to suffer their economic exploitation, social marginalization, and internal conflicts for survival.

Later, some brothers of the 'Caserio' began attending the church. Whilst they were accepted with joy, soon it was noticed that they were not respected and were even discriminated against. They did not understand many parts of the doctrine. The themes addressed in the sermons did not respond to their experiences and the activities were designed for middle class people only. Many preferred to continue with the meeting only in the 'Caserio'. Although they knew about home Bible study, in the church they did not receive support or encouragement and that made JJ think that something was very wrong.

Other situations started to complicate his work in the church, which later on made him leave and go live in Buenos Aires, Argentina. However, in this congregation he learned about the initiative led by the Spirit to open new spaces and reach others with the love of God. He was also learning more about Christ and the Scriptures. He learned to love the Word of God and study it assiduously because of the responsibility he had while teaching. JJ was already preaching in the church when he was barely 19 years old. Despite his young age, he organized three weekly home meetings with the families of the 'Caserio', with young people from his neighbourhood and from a rough neighbourhood. He saw God touching hearts of these young, rough people, with whom he had fought on the street a year ago, and they were getting to know Christ. Even today, 25 years later, when he visits Lima, they are still walking in God's ways.

His parents encouraged him to get a better academic degree. The Theology Diploma he obtained was a 3-years' course and the training was very basic. So he joined the Evangelical Seminary of Lima, and studied missiology, an area of study co-ordinated by Ruben 'Tito' Paredes. Samuel

Escobar was one of the teachers and mentors. In the seminary, people with doctorates dressed like the rest, ate with them in the dining room, played soccer, and discussed their aspirations and missionary searches. It was a time of great blessing for JJ because he was supported theologically and ministerially after feeling very lonely in the church.

A significant break in his life began here when he was 21 years old. JJ remembered reading in the buses from home to the seminary. To read Mision Integral by Rene Padilla three times in one year was a comfort. The fundamentalist Protestant perspective had put many questions into his head and knowing that others thought this way, and that they were also speaking on God's behalf, did him much good.

In 1990, he decided to study at the Buenos Aires International Baptist Theological Seminary. JJ knew that the seminary was open to the FTL (Latin American Theological Fellowship) teachers at that time. Mervin Brenemann, Paul Deiros, and Samuel Escobar taught there. It was there that he had the privilege of studying with these great teachers and meeting Rene Padilla to whom he was assigned as assistant in a bi-monthly class on Latin American Christology. He left the classes with his head full of ideas, questions, and new formulations.

On his arrival in Buenos Aires, he looked for a local church. He got to know the 'Iglesia Bautista de Constitución' and he has been part of this congregation ever since. Participating in church life in Argentina, he also learnt a lot more about Christian ministry than he was used to seeing in fundamentalist churches. He also became aware of cultural prejudices towards Peruvian citizens that put him on the other side of the road. Previously, he had lived as one who helped the marginalized, from his middle class position. In Buenos Aires, he was considered a foreigner and in many ways inferior because he was a half-breed. Words such as 'negrito' made him feel what it meant to be marginalized. The police arrested him for 'possessing a face', for appearing criminal, simply because he dressed differently or had a darker skin. Even in the seminary or the church, he was 'the Peruvian', and although it was not always said disparagingly, it indicated an inferior status and certain suspicions about him because of his nationality or his ethnic group.

He continued in that church and once he had finished his Masters in Theology in the New Testament, the church invited him to be their pastor. His initial work as a pastor was to rethink the whole process of discipleship in the church. The focus on classes and Sunday lessons stopped and a new focus started with daily work, real life encounters, service, friendship and community work. The enthusiasm was great because the church was coming out of a great crisis, having had three pastors in a two years' span. This was a church that had been asleep in the institutionalization of religion, morality and Christian life. However, this numbness was ending because the Spirit of God dwelt among them and led them down new paths that they wanted to follow.

Because JJ had different perspectives than the usual discipleship manuals, he started writing a series of Bible studies on discipleship for two people, a teacher and disciple. The methodology was based on the popular reading of the Bible, starting with life and leading to life. The Bible was the centre and Jesus of Nazareth was their vital model. JJ was strongly impressed by the work of the Spirit in their hearts, in the study of God's Word and the rediscovery of Jesus of Nazareth.

Between 1989 and 1999 Argentina underwent a government crisis. Indiscriminate privatizations dismantled the country and left thousands of families homeless. The 'Constitución' Baptist Church building was located in the city centre, two blocks away from one of the major train stations. They received people who were literally on the street. Many families, whose only income came from the sale of the house, were left homeless when the husband was fired. Flexible working and massive lay-offs, union dismemberment, businesses sold, and facilities for foreign multinationals, all ruined the domestic industry, and corruption in the courts ruined the country. As a church, they began to accommodate people and families in the building while they helped them settle somewhere. Soon they received a statement from the Baptist Convention warning them that due to legal risks they did not have authorization to do this, but they paid no attention and continued using their congregational independence. People felt cold, especially boys and girls, and elderly people. The church organized a dining room, the 'Sunday School' classrooms became rooms and at one point they were hosting more than 30 people. Soon they noticed that some government organizations and other churches called them to ask for help regarding accommodation. So, they started working on Buenos Aires city networks: Catholic institutions, non-governmental organisations (NGOs), various evangelical institutions and others institutions linked to central government. They began to assist with housing, food, health, and legal procedures to families and seniors in crisis. Everything was being transformed.

WALKING IN HIS STEPS AS OUR REFORMATION CONTINUES

We continue to walk in Jesus' footsteps when we obediently mould our lives into His teaching in a lifestyle as radical followers of Christ.

In a few years, this church was a community of faith composed of people from different nationalities. Brothers and sisters from neighbouring countries: Chile, Paraguay, Uruguay, Bolivia, Brazil, Peru, Ecuador, North America, and a growing group of brothers from Africa: Liberia and Ghana, amongst others. They decided that all voices should be heard and experienced in an inclusive church organization. Thus, church life was organized around communion, times to share meals, to pray and study the Scripture together; their lives, their model of preaching changed. Even the building changed. God touched people's hearts to open their homes and their lives; to share their goods, and to intercede for the weak before law enforcement agencies. And the most beautiful thing was that everybody was included.

Enthusiasm led some to participate actively, but others, when they saw where things were going, that it was not simply an 'integration' of the 'social' to the 'evangelization' but a holistic change that involved much more and required true conversion, were discouraged. In spite of this, JJ testifies to the fact that he has never seen God's provision to the extent that he has seen it since becoming open to being poor. They do not have bank accounts or savings. The church decided that they would not spend substantial sums in buildings; instead, the offerings would go to the people. And yet, when it was needed, their hands, their work, their offerings have supported the building that is used to shelter people, and serves as a meeting space. Together they wanted to make this place 'theirs' and evidence of this inclusion has been the care of everyone, even the people on the streets in the neighbourhood. It is beautiful to hear them use 'we', 'our' ... when they feel they are community helping one another. God has been faithful.

WALKING IN HIS STEPS IN DISCIPLESHIP TOGETHER

We walk further in the footsteps of Jesus in a combination of both ways described above: through the work of God in us, and through our personal willingness to recognize Christ as Lord over all.

It is always a journey. The church is a dream, a vision of God that we search for. That is why it is often said that if we consider the church in terms of 'mission', the mission of the church is to be a church. For JJ personally, this has meant learning to listen more than to talk, being more avid to receive teaching than to teach. He hopes to be a witness of what God wants, to share His Word and trust that the Holy Spirit will persuade. But he also wants to learn, to be taught, to see, to be. In this approach of being together and persuading and encouraging everyone, they have gone through different stages and walking as a church has taken them to exalt a specific quality: patience or perseverance.

This is how the discipleship process, in this church, has become a walk together. There are no hyper-active leaders or ones that act like bulldozers that are always in front in the work of the church. The leaders are neither pragmatic nor activists. They do not want to shine; they do not 'shine themselves.' They are muddy, dirty, tired ... but God works though them and in them to change their tastes, and their enjoyment comes from deeper things. Perhaps because their contents are not so systematized they lose some things; but they win more. A narrative theology is about living life as a narrative, sharing Christ, walking the street where, for example, a divorced person wanders back home after 'visiting' his/her children because the law says he/she is a provider. Their arms have a lot of work giving out hugs, their ears listen more, and their tables are bigger to fit more people. That is the discipleship they have emphasized. Discipleship as a narrative where they are open to be watched and accompanied, to agree with each other and devotedly look at the testimony of Jesus of Nazareth and no other. Life as a theological narrative is not lived in a hurry, for it always has time; its schedule is not full of events, nor full of plans, nor financial budgets. This theological narrative walks on roads and is a place. Its life is in the Kingdom that is coming and cannot be reached but is expected in hope against hope.

WAY OUT

JJ's part in all this is to disappear gradually. And though it hurts and takes time, he seeks to lessen himself by welcoming the Spirit, because stepping back is not easy. He makes himself dispensable by being disseminated in the community. But will he be able to continue with this trend? He hopes so.

As a community, they have re-read life in the light of the Gospels. They have been impacted by the Spirit of Christ and they run the risks of being holistic, seeking evangelization, questioning class differences, ecclesial and personal economy, the conceptions of gender, violence, injustice, civil rights, sins, ensuring the priorities of life, pastoral patience, and the commitment to stay are present holistically. They are not a community that can be called numerous. They have not had time for that. The errors, the loneliness, the loss of friends along the way, all still hurt. There still are questions, doubts that can get intense at times regarding their choices to go to those places and to make the road their place. Perhaps it is part of the faith to have doubts, to be conscious of the mistakes made and to know that they will keep coming.

Perhaps Maxi's smile as he sits in JJ's office while he shares these lines motivates him. With a swollen belly, he is proposing options for today's dinner. Recently bathed and with a touch of dignity, Maxi proposes to eat a 'guisito' although the weather is hot. He has a big appetite because he has not eaten in a long time. But even bigger is his loneliness. 'He is missing some players' --a euphemism used to say he is crazy. He makes every effort to be a part, to be loved: he does not yet know that he is already part of them and that they love him very much. What happens is that love becomes something strange for someone who has suffered so many years of indifference. But his laughter is enough for JJ. Is Juan Jose wrong? Sometimes he does not know. More than being a theologian, he wanted to be a pastor, and more than a pastor, a brother walking in the steps of Jesus. Maybe he will be able to do that. Maybe he will continue on that road.

DAVID BUSSAU
FAITH AND SOCIAL ENTREPRENEURSHIP

MAKONEN GETU

Makonen Getu is currently the Vice President of Programme Assessment and Chief Transformation Officer at Edify and serves on the OCMS Council as a Trustee.

We live and work with people who do bad and good things. We can learn to do bad things from bad examples. Or we can learn and do good things from good examples. Whatever we choose to be and do, we, in turn, set examples to others. We are constantly influenced and influence for the bad and good. As we do so, we destroy or build.

David Bussau grew up in an orphanage and became a God-fearing entrepreneur at the age of 15 and then a co-Founder of Opportunity International, a Christian micro-finance organization providing micro-finance services to over 6 million economically active poor. I have related with David as my leader, co-worker and friend for over one and a half decades and I feel blessed to have the opportunity of sharing with you some of the important lessons I have drawn from his work and life story. At 71, David is still in active ministry and a lot more is yet to come. This paper is about the influence of faith on David's life and work and the examples his journey so far has set before us. David's story is inherently igniting and empowering and brings a glimpse of hope. I will focus on the following five lessons.

THE WAY THINGS BEGIN IS NOT NECESSARILY THE WAY THEY END

David was born in a poor working-class neighbourhood in Wellington, South New Zealand in November 1940.[2] David's father abandoned the family and left for Auckland before David turned 8 and he never saw him again. Being poor and single, his mother was in no way able to provide support to four children and decided to leave David and his younger brother at the Anglican boys' home. After being abandoned just before he turned 9, David saw his mother only once and never again. The general environment at the orphanage was abusive and hostile to empowerment and self-confidence. The boys were constantly made to believe that there was no other hope for them than working as farm workers and labourers and David was reminded of his lowly position with jarring regularity. In David's own words, 'there was a perception that we were delinquents who wouldn't amount to much'[3]. This prejudice-filled treatment of the boys caused some of them to go into violence and crime.

According to Tyndale's account, David overcame the oppressive and disempowering environment leading him into self-destruction by developing tenacity and creatively inventing survival means. He was naturally entrepreneurial and liked hard work. He grabbed any opportunity he could to work. Patience, tolerance, kindness, resilience and determination to be free and independent were some of the qualities he developed early in his life at the boys' home. He was also athletic and showed leadership in this area.

David left school at the age of 15 to start his own business with a rented hotdog stand in Auckland, New Zealand. This business flourished quickly to 15 hotdog stands. He sold this and moved into the restaurant business, which also flourished. He sold that and moved to Australia and started a construction business that became successful. In 1974, David moved to Darwin to help the victims devastated by Cyclone Tracy. In 1976, he volunteered to move to Indonesia to build houses for displaced people, churches and dams in response to the earthquake crisis that destroyed houses, temples, schools and hospitals and killed hundreds of people. During his time there, he started lending small amounts of his own money to micro-entrepreneurs to help them alleviate their poverty through the creation of employment and income. David saw this working as people were repaying their loans and experiencing improvements in their lives. Encouraged by this positive development, David founded the Maranatha Trust (MT) in 1979 to mobilize funding to expand the lending programme he started in Indonesia.

In the same year, David came into contact with Al Whitaker[4], an American Christian businessman, who had expanded his Latin-America-based enterprise development programme to Indonesia. After working together under their respective organizations for about 10 years, the two co-founded Opportunity International in 1988. Today, Opportunity runs a microfinance programme focused on outreach, sustainability and transformation serving a total of over 6 million poor loan clients, depositors and insurance holders and operating a loan portfolio of about $

600 million in 23 developing countries and is one of the leading and reputable global micro-finance organizations. David has also been instrumental in the formation of many other global organizations, including OCMS.

As participants in the global Opportunity micro-finance programmes, millions of financially excluded poor people have been enabled to access financial and training services they needed for sustaining and creating jobs and generating income for themselves and their families. Although not all those who benefited from the Opportunity operations have fully escaped poverty, they have been able to survive with less suffering and more opportunities to educate and feed their children and to improve their overall well-being, including spiritual transformation. This was a noble achievement made in response to Jesus's call to feed the hungry, give shelter to the homeless and give water to the thirsty, as recorded in Matthew 25.

Building God's church has been David's other passion. In 1999, he founded the Wholistic Transformational Resource Center whose vision is 'to see strong local churches that are self-sustaining, effectively witnessing the whole gospel'. The aim is to equip, unite and strengthen the Christian body in their task to empower members of the church community through transformational and holistic MED programmes.[5]

Over the last 10 years, David has earned 12 different national and international awards in recognition of his achievements and contributions to humankind, particularly the poor.[6] David has also authored and co-authored several books and pamphlets.[7]

The intention of making this incomplete list of achievements and recognitions is not to present David as a great achiever and to see him through his achievements. In fact, David would not like to see me doing this as he believes that it is what we *do not do* rather than what we are achieving that is important. The purpose is to demonstrate that the way things start is not necessarily the way they end.

Very often, it is perceived that people with good beginnings such as being born into well-to-do families, with a good education, good upbringing, and safe environment will have good end results. On the contrary, those who are born into poor families, who have limited education, poor upbringing, and an abusive environment, are assumed to end up faring badly or even getting worse. David's story is another living testimony that the way things begin is not necessarily the way they end. Poor or humble beginnings do not necessarily lead to bad ends. Going by the conventional perception, David's childhood hardships were likely to condemn him to self-destruction. On the contrary, he creatively used his sad situation as an opportunity of sharpening, disciplining and preparing himself for the future. He chose to look forward and not backward and rose to glory against all odds. He was once abandoned, forgotten, downtrodden, oppressed and despised. Now he is recognized as a global change leader. The message: Things don't necessarily have to end the way they begin.

David's journey is also an example of God's plan for his life. As much as his personal effort contributed to his rise to significance, it would have not been possible without his faith in God and God's faithfulness to him. The fatherless David embraced God as his father as soon as he heard his Sunday school teacher talk about how God cared for children abandoned by their parents. God knew and had a plan for David before he was born and to keep him and take him out of the boys' home. David believed and God responded. The lesson here is: What God did for David, He will do for all who believe and are obedient.

The other example is that God rewards those who serve others. Those who give their resources and themselves for the good of others receive from God. Giving is receiving. *'He who has pity on the poor lends to the Lord, and He will pay back what he has given'* (Proverbs 19:17). David is not a person who seeks to promote himself or is worried about taking credit. He often avoids high tables and being in the limelight. All he seeks to do is give his resources, time, energy, and passion for the service of others and God's Kingdom. In return, as the last become first, God has raised him to what we call higher ground. The global recognitions and awards he has been able to receive over the years are awards from God and David receives them as such. The message: Those who serve others to the glory of God will be honoured by God as David has been.

RELEASING IS THE KEY TO MAKING PEOPLE

Jesus said, 'follow me and I will make you fishers of men.' (Matthew 4:9) and 'go therefore and make disciples of all the nations, baptizing them in the name of the Father and of the Son and of the Holy Spirit, teaching them to observe all things that I have commanded you' (Matthew 28:19-20).

David followed Jesus and was made a fisher of men. However, he did not do it the traditional way by planting churches and preaching the gospel. He did it the business way, using the entrepreneurship skills and experience God enabled him to gain as a young boy and creating jobs and income which set him free from poverty and dependency, as narrated in the above section. Instead of planting physical church infrastructures as his core focus, he planted businesses. Instead of bringing people to Christ by preaching from the pulpit, he did so through board rooms, business conferences, business training and one-on-one discipleship of business leaders and micro-entrepreneurs. Instead of bringing half the gospel by focusing on evangelization, he brought the whole gospel by offering both the word and bread, thereby meeting both the material and spiritual aspects of life. He demonstrated business was mission in its own right and that businessmen and women were missionaries.

Through his businesses, Maranatha Trust, Opportunity International, WTRC and Churches, David has recruited, trained, mentored, and nurtured countless numbers of leaders and organizations of all types and levels across the globe with the aim of generating Kingdom outcomes. However, it is not the number that stands out as anything particular but the approach he applies to make (develop) people. He applies the Jesus way of releasing people.

In realizing his model of making people (leadership), David has evolved what he calls the 5 Ps of potential: (i) See potential – you see it and feel it in a person, (ii) Buy potential – you pay for it, (iii) Sow potential – invest in people, (iv) Build potential – nurture people, (v) Leverage potential – release them.[8]

The crux of David's release model is the recognition that God has created us as His image bearers and with potential and that He trusts our ability in fulfilling His purpose. He first sees our potential and strengths which are from and in Him. He addresses our weaknesses by first looking at our potential and gives us responsibilities knowing that we will do it with His enabling power.[9]

The first thing David sees in a person is what that person has and sensing what he/she can potentially do and not what he/she does not have and not able to do. He sees and treats people not as they are but as what they can become and then gives them responsibilities. By doing that he expresses his trust and confidence in people, both of which are critical in the creation of self-worth and dignity.

The other releasing approach David applies is that he takes a facilitative role. David is a man of fewer words, a man slow to speak and quick to listen. He says less and listens more. He asks and informs more and commands less. He is not an impositionist nor is he an interventionist. He rather applies a 'hands off' approach and lets people go on with their tasks and comes in when necessary and offers every needed support. As someone says, 'he cheers from the side-lines and then dives in when the going gets really rough'.

Still more important in his approach is his personality – his being. He presents himself as a lowly person, who is easy to approach and to attract his attention. His personality and his humble way of approaching and relating with people release people. He hardly talks about his status or achievements. He does not play big in anyway. If you do not know who he is, he does not give you any help in that area of detection.

Vulnerability and integrity are other qualities of David's releasing leadership model. Very often, it is not only what we say and do that have impact on people around us. It is also how we carry ourselves. When we act and relate with people with vulnerability and integrity, we release them.[10] 'I am gentle and lowly in heart' (Matthew 11:29) said Jesus. By following Jesus's example, David creates a secure environment for people, no matter their social status, and releases them and lightens their burden.

JESUS-DRIVEN LIFE GENERATES BOLDNESS AND FREEDOM

My experience of David is that Jesus is at the heart of his life and work. He seeks to live, work and breathe Jesus. His core motivation is the recognition and acceptance of the gifts that God has given him and the conviction that those gifts need to be used to sow into the lives of others and to build the Kingdom.

David also displays boldness. He is not afraid of doing anything anywhere to fulfil the mission of Jesus: setting the captives free wherever he senses the Holy Spirit leads him. Very often, David chooses to do ministry not in easy but difficult and unreachable environments. A good example is the micro-enterprise development programme he started in North Korea in 2003. He did this for the purpose of sowing God's love through business in that difficult country.[11]

Moreover, David does not allow to be constrained by strategic plans in serving people. His principle is to serve people first and foremost and not programmes. He is sensitive to what people want and not what his strategic plans say. Being a good listener, David often amends written programmes to meet needs and unlock potential.

What is the source of David's boldness? It is not his physical strength or stamina. It is not his knowledge and competence. It is the recognition that the power that is in him is greater than the one in the world. His boldness does not emanate from reliance on his ability but from reliance on his faith in Jesus. His confidence and dependency on Christ give him flexibility and freedom to serve without fear and constraints. He models the 'I-decrease-and-He-increases' principle of John the Baptist.

WORKING TO LIVE AND NOT LIVING TO WORK

God worked six days to create what we needed for our life and rested on the seventh day thereby setting an example of how we should treat to work and live. He wants us to work and co-create the things we want for sustaining our lives from the resources He bestowed. At the same time, He does not want us to treat work as everything in life. He also wants us to have leisure time – time to relate and time to rest. He wants us to live a balanced life – to work to live and not live to work. In other words, to live is the purpose and to work is the means.

David is a good example of living this out. As much as he respects and values the importance of work in the creation of livelihoods and devotes a great deal of his time to work, he also respects and values the importance of leisure in the creation of a holistic, balanced, life.

In translating his conviction into practice, David combines hard work with sports and quality time with family. He plays squash, tennis, jogs and swims. He also makes sure that he has adequate and quality time for socializing with family and other people. It must be said that the balancing of the two has happened more in the latter part of his life. To use his own words, he has changed from a human 'doing' to a human 'being' over time. All 'doing' is not about working, of course. David's point here refers to the latter.[12]

The message here is that we need to live a more balanced and purposeful life. We do not idolize work and spend our lives just working and working, doing and doing as many hours per day as we can but also being and relating. As the South African saying goes, human beings are human beings through other human beings. Doing and being in a balanced way is what we should seek in life.

We All Have Weaknesses

The lessons presented above draw on David's strengths: faith, humility, passion, influence, love, care, discipline, loyalty. In short, David's story is inherently igniting and empowering. It heals and brings light and hope. However, like all human beings, David has weaknesses too, some of which contradict his strong traits:

- Is too much of an independent worker and often difficult to manage in a team situation.
- Is stubborn and often times have to learn things the hard way.
- Tends to sacrifice efficiency for a higher purpose.
- Is too pragmatic.
- Does not always think through the consequences.
- Does not work to a formula.
- Struggles with dealing with bureaucracies/red tape, public speaking, compliance and seven-course Chinese banquet.
- Is impatient – sees a problem and seeks to solve it quickly.

Other Voices – Concluding with Other People's Experiences of David's Impact

At critical points, he encouraged and released me to find the right solutions and continue to make commitments in the face of uncertainty. He has demonstrated a mature faith and understanding of human nature, whatever the culture.

His influence has shaped all we do in the realm of giving, how we see development and our role in this world.... He has modeled how to serve God in every area of our lives – in work, finances, relationships, time, family.

It has made me see potential in every person I encounter just like he saw the potential in me. He has made me see the value of mentoring and its role in relationships. He mentored me and made me grow and now I want to pass that on too.

His example of following Christ has been the greatest influence in my commitment and journey. His example of serving the God-given potential and purpose on people's lives and communities has shaped my understanding and life's work.

The secret to my active and long life is having a son-in-law like David.

How I wish I can be like David, a visionary man, an inspiration, a motivator, true Christian.

BIBLIOGRAPHY

Bussau, D. (1998) *Reflections on Christian Microenterprise Development*. Sydney: Opportunity International Australia.

Bussau, D. & Samuel, V. (1998) *How Then Should We Lend? A Biblical Validation of Microenterprise Development*. Sydney: Opportunity International Australia.

Bussau, D. & Mask, R. (2000) *Christian Microenterprise Development: A Handbook*. Manila: Christian Transformation Resource Center.

Bussau, D. & Getu, M. (2003) *Wealth Generation & Kingdom Building Through CMED: A Biblical Reflection*. Manila: Christian Transformation Resource Center.

Bussau, D. & Getu, M. (2003) *Sustainable Transformational Development: A Diagnostic Tool*. Manila: Christian Transformation Resource Center.

Tyndale, P. (2004) *Do Not Look Back: The David Bussau Story: How an Abandoned Child Became a Champion of the Poor*. Crows Nest: Allen and Unwin.

PETER KUZMIČ
A BELIEVING AND PRACTISING SCHOLAR IN THE SERVICE OF THE KINGDOM

CORNELIU CONSTANTINEANU

Corneliu Constantineanu serves as the President and Associate Professor of New Testament Studies at Institutul Teologic Penticostal, Bucharest, Romania.

A SHORT BIOGRAPHICAL NARRATIVE

It is a great honour and joy for me to make a presentation on Dr. Peter Kuzmič's life and work. I have had the privilege of having Professor Kuzmič as a mentor, colleague and friend for more than twenty years. He remains one of the most persistent, positive influences in my life, an example of a life radically shaped by the Gospel of reconciliation and love. Respected as one of the most distinguished evangelical scholars and Christian leaders in Central and Eastern Europe, he is an internationally recognized authority on the subject of Christian ministry in a post-Communist context.

Currently, Dr. Kuzmič is the President of the Evangelical Theological Seminary in Osijek, Croatia and also the Eva B. and Paul E. Tomas Distinguished Professor of World Missions and European Studies at Gordon-Conwell Theological Seminary, MA, USA. He is married to Vlasta and has three daughters and 5 grandchildren.

Peter Kuzmič was born on June 26, 1946, in Slovenia – a small Republic of the Former Yugoslavia – in a family whose ancestor, Štefan Kuzmič, 'had participated in the small Slovenian Reformation movement by translating the New Testament into Vendish, the native tongue of Prekmurje, in 1771' (Tatjana Kuzmič). From his youth, Peter had an inquisitive mind and a great love for books. He began his theological education at a German evangelical school and then completed with honours his B.A. (Southern California College, Costa Mesa, 1971) and M.A. (Wheaton Graduate School of Theology, USA, 1972). It was in 1972, based on his outstanding master thesis, that Peter Kuzmič received a full scholarship for his doctorate at Harvard University. However, the

Communist government back in Yugoslavia granted an unprecedented permission for opening a theological school and so Peter has given up his scholarship at Harvard and returned to establish and lead Biblical-Theological Institute (BTI) in Zagreb. While in Zagreb, Peter Kuzmič was accepted to study at the Catholic Faculty of Theology as the first Protestant at that institution to obtain a M.Th. (1975) and a PhD. (1980) from a Catholic institution.

If most of Peter's activity focused on the development of the seminary, it is also true that from the mid-1980s he was in great demand as an international speaker and as a courageous voice of Christianity behind the Iron Curtain. He has spoken internationally, including plenary addresses at Lausanne II, Urbana, the European Leadership Consultation and the National Association of Evangelicals Fiftieth Anniversary. Dr. Kuzmič is a member of the Lausanne Committee for World Evangelization and many other boards. With the outbreak of the war in former Yugoslavia, Peter's life would change significantly as he became deeply involved – not only in speaking against the atrocities during the war but especially in the humanitarian relief that was so much needed in the early 1990s. Thus, Dr. Kuzmič founded Agape, a humanitarian relief organization, which, along with New Europe Vision, which he also founded, ministers to the physical and spiritual needs of those in the Balkans. He was influential in bringing about the Dayton Peace Awards and served as an advisor on reconciliation for national leaders in the Balkans, the United Nations and the U.S. State Department. He has received the Presidential Award of Croatia and the Helsinki Award for Human Rights and Religious Liberty in recognition of his work in promoting inter-religious dialogue.

After this brief overview of the most important elements of his biography, I would like to present his life and ministry under four headings which best capture his comprehensive engagements in the field of theological education, Christian mission, scholarship and public life. These are also the areas in which Peter Kuzmič has contributed significantly and left an enduring legacy. These are some of the most important lessons we learn from his life and ministry.

Theological Education: Peter Kuzmič as Teacher, Mentor and Visionary

Most people who have known Dr. Kuzmič would agree that when it comes to theological education he is a dedicated teacher, a beloved mentor and a truly inspiring visionary. Generations of students have learned from his wisdom, have been inspired by his comprehensive vision and have grown under his mentorship to become today's leaders. Indeed, through a unique and holistic approach to theological education that he gave to the Evangelical Theological Seminary in Osijek, he has contributed significantly to shaping the face of theological education in Central and Eastern Europe.

For people in the West, with long traditions of Evangelical theological reflection, it may not be a spectacular thing. But for post-Communist Eastern Europe, the church just came out of 45 years of oppression and persecution (or infiltrations and control by the authorities) by the Communist regime, and so the first priority of the church was survival. Immediately after the collapse of the Iron Curtain, the greatest need was for basic and practical training of church workers. And yet, Peter Kuzmič was among the few who insisted for the great need to begin and sustain serious theological reflection and training in the specific post-Communist context of this part of the world.

In the 40 years of activity of the school, Peter Kuzmič has managed to build a distinctive and unique ethos characterized by: 1) Academic Excellence; 2) Christian Spiritual Formation; 3) Relevance to Modern Society; 4) Transdenominational Awareness; and 5) Multicultural Education. By embodying all these aspects into the everyday life of the school, the students received an integrative, holistic understanding of education and of Christian mission in the world. He insisted that in the complex world we live today, the churches around the world need leaders who have a holistic understanding of reality, who are trained to engage deeply in the world, with all its aspects of cultures and societies; leaders who are able to offer Christian, biblically-based alternatives to the many problems of this world.

It was due to his vision for serious theological study that he built one of the best theological libraries in that part of the world, a library that today houses upwards of 100,000 volumes! ETS in Osijek was the first school in Eastern Europe, and remained the only one for many years, to offer a master's programme in theology. Today, there are several heads of theological schools in Romania, Ukraine, Moldova, Russia, Serbia, and Macedonia who were theologically trained at Peter Kuzmič's school in Osijek.

Dr. Kuzmič's commitment to Christian education is further underscored by his tenure as Chairman of the Council of East-European Theological Education as well as his service for a number of years as Chair of the Board of the Oxford Centre for Mission Studies.

SCHOLARSHIP: PETER KUZMIČ AS THEOLOGIAN, MISSIOLOGIST, ETHICIST

Although by education Dr. Kuzmič is an expert in Slavic translations of the Bible, his interests and calling have led him to explore a wider territory and to contribute significantly to other areas of theological inquiry. As the Eva B. and Paul E. Toms Distinguished Professor of World Missions and European Studies at Gordon-Conwell Theological Seminary in USA, Dr. Kuzmič is known for his insistence on 'holistic mission' and for his involvement with various representative international theological circles, such as the World Evangelical Alliance, where he served as Chair of the Theological Commission. An award-winning writer, Dr. Kuzmič has authored eight books and hundreds of articles, as well as contributions to numerous compendia, handbooks and encyclopaedias. In addition to writing, he has served on the editorial advisory boards of several academic journals, including the *European Journal of Theology* and the *Journal of Pentecostal Theology*, and was the founding editor of *Izvori*, a Croatian interdenominational monthly. In recognition of his scholarly contributions, he has received the Merrill C. Tenney Award for New Testament Scholarship and an honorary D.D. from Asbury Theological Seminary. Dr. Kuzmič is listed in *Who's Who in Biblical Studies and Archaeology*.

He always likes to define himself as a 'task theologian'. For him, theology was not simply an intellectual exercise but rather a serious biblical and theological reflection on the crucial issues facing the mission of the church in every generation, in every context. To describe in three words the essence of Dr. Kuzmič's legacy in this area, I would choose these: '*Believing* and *Practising Scholars*.' He is a Christian leader with a strong faith in God as the only one who can finally bring the Kingdom of God; a leader with a great passion for God, for the world and for people; a man of God who embodied the gospel in everyday circumstances of life, and articulated it in contemporary, relevant language and categories. He will remain as an example of a leader who was able to integrate his beliefs, praxis and scholarship into a holistic vision of Christian life and ministry.

Christian Leadership and Ministry: Peter Kuzmič as Pastor, Evangelist, Global Leader

In his country, Dr. Kuzmič is known as a preacher, minister, pastor and as former president of the Evangelical/Pentecostal Church in Yugoslavia and subsequently in Croatia, as well as the president of the Protestant Evangelical Council of Croatia. Most significantly, however, is his crucial role in establishing and leading the humanitarian relief organization 'Agape' as a response to the devastating effects of the war in former Yugoslavia. Through this ministry, he has helped thousands of refugees and people affected by this destructive conflict.

During and after the war in the former Yugoslavia, under the leadership of Peter Kuzmič, the Protestant churches acted very courageously for peace and unity among the different ethnic groups:

> *While the Orthodox priests blessed the Serbian soldiers going to war, starting in the summer of 1991, and the Catholic priests blessed the Croatian soldiers, Peter Kuzmič organized several reconciliation meetings for the Yugoslav Protestants in Hungary. For his efforts in reconciliation and humanitarian engagement, Peter was awarded the Order of Danica of Croatia in 1998 by the first president of post-Yugoslav Croatia.*
>
> *Risking his life, Peter visited Osijek several times to witness the course of events in person and identify what kind of help was needed. The enormous list of contacts he had established in the West and his reputation as a pro-democratic promoter of human rights and religious liberties proved extremely helpful at the time when the rest of Europe and the United States could only watch in horror at the kind of violence evocative of World War II.*
>
> *The suffering of the refugees propelled Peter to found a humanitarian organization called Agape, which distributed hot meals, dried food articles, hygiene items, medical supplies, clothing, blankets and more not only in Croatia, but also in Bosnia, which experienced violence on a grander and much longer scale than did Croatia, and later on, also in Kosovo. Agape was so effective that it was nominated for the $1,000,000.00 Hilton prize. Later on, when Agape was the first organization to distribute aid in the recently liberated Bosnian town of*

> *Bihać, Peter half-jokingly asked the mayor how come the two of them – a Christian and a Muslim – hit it off so well —'That is because you are not the kind of Christian we Muslims typically envision, the mayor replied seriously, —and because I am not the type of Muslim that you Christians typically envision – a statement worth dwelling upon even more today and on a global scale. (Tatjana Kuzmič)*

Beyond Croatia, Dr. Kuzmič was founder and Chairman of the Board of the Fellowship of European Evangelical Theologians, founder and Chair of International Fellowship of Evangelical Mission Theologians (INFEMIT), and is one of the leading evangelical theologians who have been associated with the Lausanne Movement from its very beginnings in 1974. Together with Phillip Hogan and Dr. Yonggi Cho, he founded the World Assemblies of God Fellowship and its humanitarian arm WAGRA. Other leadership roles include activity in the World Evangelical Theological Commission and the International Board of AD 2000 & Beyond.

FAITH AND PUBLIC LIFE: PETER KUZMIČ AS ANALYST, SPEAKER, PROPHET

For Peter Kuzmič, faith has never been something limited to the spiritual dimension of existence. Rather, faith relates to and addresses life in its totality as it is lived in the midst of culture and society. How could anyone forget his repeated reminder – following none other than Karl Barth in this – that we should hold the Bible in one hand and the newspaper in the other! And it is precisely because he did not teach only in the classroom but also by his own life and example that he managed to inspire a holistic vision for Christian life, an authentic passion for the Kingdom of God, and a genuine love for God's people and God's world.

He insists on active Christian engagement with society in order to model an alternative to contemporary patterns of thinking and modes of living. An example of his deep concern with how the gospel speaks to the contemporary world is his commitment, for more than a decade, to writing a bi-monthly column in one of the leading Croatian newspapers, in which he analyzes, speaks to and prophetically challenges all aspects of social, political, religious and moral life. A highlight of his public engagement is his role in the Dayton Peace Accord and his membership in the Croatian Helsinki Committee for Human Rights. In recognition of his significant contribution to a culture of peaceful inter-religious, multi-ethnic, inter-cultural dialogue, he has received the Presidential Award of Croatia for Peace-making in 1999, as well as the Helsinki Award for Human Rights and Religious Liberty. Recent awards from the City of Osijek include the Outstanding Citizen Award in 2000 and the Lifetime Achievement Award in 2008.

This understanding and promotion of the public dimension of faith has been a distinctive aspect of Dr. Kuzmič's ministry. His effort is particularly significant in today's pluralistic context, in which Christians leaders must find appropriate ways not simply to cope with 'otherness' and 'difference' but to engage, with their congregations, in the public square, in order to promote a culture of dialogue, respect and love. This subject has always been very close to the heart of Professor Kuzmič, namely, a holistic understanding of Christian life and mission, an integrative understanding of the gospel as public truth – concerned with and addressing the entire reality.

In sum, Peter Kuzmič's legacy is that of man of God, consumed by an inextinguishable passion for the Kingdom of God and whose life of intense activity and diverse engagements is an example of a disciple of Jesus Christ, a true believing and practising Scholar. Throughout his life, Peter Kuzmič has emphasized that the gospel is the extraordinary good news of God for the redemption of the entire creation and so it is to be fully integrated into the realities of life, so that the effective and transforming power of the gospel is made manifest. He insists and illustrates that in his own life that when a person responds to the gospel one is bound to follow the logic of that gospel and live accordingly. In a world in which there is a sharp dichotomy between faith and life, between theology and ethics, Peter's legacy encourages us to recover a biblical view of the 'obedience of faith', of an authentic and radical discipleship and of a truly prophetic engagement in society as a manifestation of the lordship of Christ over every aspect of life.

By his own life and example, Peter Kuzmič has inspired many to capture a holistic vision of the Kingdom of God, a passion for God, His world, and His people. Through his life and ministry, he has constantly challenged those who had the privilege to cross his way, to devote their lives to profound study, prayer, and authentic Christian living.

RONALD J. SIDER
'I AM NOT A SOCIAL ACTIVIST', BUT…

AL TIZON AND PAUL ALEXANDER

Al Tizon and Paul Alexander have been working alongside Ron Sider for the last several years as faculty colleagues at Palmer Theological Seminary of Eastern University as well as ministry colleagues at Evangelicals for Social Action, both near Philadelphia, PA. Co-Presidents of ESA, Al and Paul carry on Ron's legacy as they advance ESA's holistic ministry, public policy and cultural transformational initiatives throughout the world. [13]

Two pictures hanging in Ron's Sider's office attest to a remarkable journey. One is of Ron outdoors sporting a fishing vest and hat, smiling proudly from ear to ear, as he holds up a trophy catch. It looks like a salmon or a steelhead. The picture shows Ron the fisherman, the outdoorsman; it conveys serenity and simplicity, as well as adventure.

Another picture shows him with several others sitting around a conference table with then-President Jimmy Carter. He and the rest of those at the table were not passively staring at the President as he gave some speech; on the contrary, the picture conveys Ron as part of a select group of theologians, ethicists, and ministers engaged and interacting with the commander-in-chief, as they discussed crucial policy matters. The picture conveys Dr. Ron Sider, the brilliant scholar, churchman, political consultant, world-changer. Seen together, these two pictures demonstrate God's use of an ordinary farm boy, who grew up in (and still enjoys) the simplicities of rural life, to accomplish extraordinary things in the ecclesial, political and cultural arenas.

A LIFE SKETCH

Ronald James Sider was born September 17, 1939 in a farmhouse near Stevensville, a small farming community in Southern Ontario, Canada. Raised in a Brethren in Christ family, Sider came to faith in childhood. 'At about eight years of age,' he recalls, 'during one of the regular revival meetings at my home congregation, I knelt at the altar and accepted Jesus Christ.'[14]

That faith was tested, however, during his undergraduate years at Waterloo College in Ontario (now Wilfrid Laurier University). If it were not for the arrival of Dr. John Warwick Montgomery to serve as the new head of the history department, Sider's faith might have been snuffed out by the winds of secularism, which were blowing fiercely at the time. Instead, with Montgomery as his inspiration, Sider set out to be an historian and an apologist in a secular university setting.

With a B.A. in history from Waterloo and his bride, Arbutus Lichti, by his side, Sider went off to Yale University to become the Renaissance-Reformation scholar that he thought God was calling him to be. Sensing the need to integrate faith with his scholarship, he took a break at the two-year mark of his doctoral studies, in order to get theological grounding at Yale's Divinity School, just up the road. He eventually completed a Bachelor of Divinity degree (the equivalent of M.Div. today), before resuming and completing his Ph.D. in history. Amid his historical and theological studies at Yale, Sider immersed himself in the work of Inter-Varsity Christian Fellowship, which provided the context for both the cultivation of his own spiritual growth and the working out of a more holistic understanding of the gospel.

The plan after Yale was to serve as a faculty advisor for IVCF while teaching history at a secular university, but a strong sense of call to renew a biblically-grounded concern for social justice, particularly for evangelicals, began to grow within him. This sense of call guided his decision to accept an invitation from Messiah College to help launch an urban campus in Philadelphia in collaboration with Temple University. Instead of applying his knowledge of theology and history in and for the academic community primarily, Sider became a popularizer, that is, a scholar who wrote for popular audiences to inspire and guide ordinary people to follow Jesus in works of compassion, justice, and evangelism.

Scholarship and Activism

He communicated this vision both through scholarship and activism. He has written over 30 books, but the one for which he is most famous (or infamous, depending on one's point of view) is the celebrated *Rich Christians in an Age of Hunger*, first published in 1977. Voted by *Christianity Today* as one of the 100 most influential books on religion in the twentieth century, *Rich Christians* has inspired and mobilized hundreds of thousands of

Christians and churches around the world to care about the poor as part and parcel of the Christian life.

His books complemented his activities, which included organizing the Thanksgiving gathering of 1973 that produced the much-lauded 'Chicago Declaration of Evangelical Social Concern.' This crucial document played its part in reawakening the evangelical social conscience, particularly in North America but also around the world. With the Chicago Declaration as the founding document, Sider launched Evangelicals for Social Action (ESA), an organization committed to maturing the evangelical social conscience. Much of Sider's work has had to do with striking a balance between social concern and evangelism, i.e., holistic ministry.

Beyond doing works of compassion and justice alongside evangelism, Sider has also championed biblically-informed politics as part of his activist work, urging Christians to embrace a non-partisan consistent life ethic that must inform the church's engagement in the body politic.

I Am Not a Social Activist

Ron Sider is associated primarily with the evangelical reawakening of social responsibility and biblically-informed political involvement, and this is not inaccurate. However, Sider's great contribution in this area is but a part of a larger vision – a vision of biblical, authentic, radical discipleship, i.e. what it means to follow Jesus Christ faithfully and prophetically in the world.

His works, which span more than four decades, have guided the faithful to engage in the church, education, culture and politics by the guiding light of the gospel and its radical implications. The influence upon others of his vision for holistic ministry and biblically-informed politics goes deep and wide. Indeed, countless Christians have been impacted by Sider's works. But more than numbers, the vision has been embraced across conventional lines, as women and men, young and old, evangelical and ecumenical, and black, white and brown have been impacted.

We are two such people, who have been greatly shaped by Ron Sider long before we ever met him. We are what we are and do what we do today largely because of his influence, and it has been a tremendous privilege for us to have worked with Ron these last several years as faculty colleagues at Palmer Theological Seminary of Eastern University and as programme directors of ESA.

PROCLAIMING JESUS IN WORD AND DEED (BY AL TIZON)

I was a promising young fundamentalist when I read Ron Sider's *Rich Christians in an Age of Hunger* in the early 1980s. Zealous to save desperate souls from the sinking ship called Planet Earth, I went off to a Christian college to prepare for the task of getting as many people into the lifeboat of Christ as I could. As far as I knew, this wholly defined the church's mission.

But then I read *Rich Christians,* along with a handful of other prophetic books. The multi-punch combination of these works knocked me off my feet, and my understanding of mission has never been the same. I got up from the floor a bit wobbly, but with a strange new clarity about God's heart for the poor and a strong resolve not to order my life according to the false promises of the American Dream.

If it was the power punches of these books that profoundly realigned my thinking in terms of compassion and justice, then it was an on-location graduate course in Central America that propelled me toward a life of action. Amid the in-your-face poverty endured by so many people whom I had the privilege to meet, the God of the poor and oppressed spoke to me in a most profound and life-changing way. I returned home persuaded that if the gospel did not address human need in the here and now, then the good news was no good at all.

I could have easily gone the way of the bleeding heart liberal activist who advocates for the poor and who sees the ultimate human problem as socio-political, but my own personal experience of desperately needing a Saviour, then and now, has prevented that. The evil that resides in my own heart, before *and* after my conversion, reminds me that the gospel is also a profoundly personal thing. It is a heart thing. It is repentance, confession and forgiveness. It is falling down and getting up again by the grace of God. Evangelism – to tell the good news in such a way that clearly invites persons to give their hearts to Christ and to join the new community – should not and must not be eclipsed by social action; just like social action should not and must not be eclipsed by evangelism. Herein lies the genius of the holistic vision that Ron Sider has championed for the past four decades. The good news of the kingdom of God touches every level of our fallen-ness, from the injustices of oppressive social structures to the sin of the human heart. If we are faithful to this gospel, then we will bear witness to it by both word and deed.

Armed with such a vision, my wife Janice and I sold most of our belongings and moved to the Philippines – my ethnic homeland – for almost a decade, as we engaged in in community development, healthcare, and evangelistic/pastoral ministries. As we worked alongside our Filipino sisters and brothers, we strove to live out the holistic vision. For both individual persons and the poor communities in which they lived needed the power of the gospel to transform them. This was true in the squatter communities that we served in the Philippines, and it remains true in the impoverished communities that we serve in America through Word & Deed Network, ESA's ministry in and through local congregations to make a difference in the lives and communities of the poor and the lost.

I credit/blame Ron Sider for doing his part in wrecking my middle-class sense of normalcy and images of success! He did this by pointing the way toward the kind of discipleship that envisions the Body of Christ – the Church – addressing the full gamut of human need toward the transformation of the world and for the glory of God.

Peace, Justice and Simplicity (by Paul Alexander)

I grew up on eighty acres in southeast Kansas in a loving family, worshiping at least three times a week in the local Assembly of God (a Pentecostal church). And unfortunately, that's where I learned most of my racist jokes. I was socialized well in the local culture and reified racism, militarism, nationalism, sexism, free market capitalism, and homophobia. I was a Jesus-loving, gun-toting, American-flag-waving, teller of racist jokes seeking to make my millions at the expense of the poor, if necessary. My parents prayed for me every day and I went on missions trips to Guatemala and Venezuela in my teen years, as well as to youth camp each summer and revivals throughout the year. While doing my M.Div. and at the start of my Ph.D., my favourite three hours each day were the Rush Limbaugh show, an extremely right-wing television talk show, because finally somebody was saying what I believed.

Then I became an atheist, and found pacifism in the history of American Pentecostalism, and was introduced to the works of John Howard Yoder, Stanley Hauerwas, and Ron Sider. Ron's *Rich Christians in an Age of Hunger* radically reoriented my understanding of wealth, accumulation, generosity, simplicity, poverty, and the gospel of Jesus Christ. I read it as a twenty-five-year-old who was using student loan money to buy rental properties. I had also borrowed $50,000 and put it in an E-Trade account, margined it to $100,000, and was day-trading during the Internet boom of the late 1990s. I was working to become rich and telling myself that I would share the wealth, while doing graduate work in theological ethics and no longer believing in God.

Although I was sceptical of *Rich Christians* and quite frankly thought it quite stupid at first, discovering Ron (along with many others like him, including many in my own faith tradition) challenged me and my 'isms' and phobias in new ways. Following the reading of *Rich Christians*, I ordered ten or so books on simplicity because it intrigued me and I wanted to learn all about it. After reading them, I realized that I should have just borrowed a book on simplicity and then shared it with someone else! Despite these books getting to me, I was still buying real estate to become a millionaire and was not yet committed to reconstructing my faith. It does not all sink in at once. In fact, it is still sinking in and I am still trying to learn how to reify other ways of life even now. This journey of faith is life-long and we experience losses and even changes of mind, heart, and direction along the way, as the Spirit works in our lives.

Ron's life has been one of prophetic challenge and invitation to both the church and society to genuine discipleship. And although we do not agree on everything (what fun would there be in that?), I am deeply thankful for the profound impact he has had on my life and on Christianity as a whole. At a crucial time in my life, his work helped me find enough courage to follow Jesus in entirely new ways, and it helped embolden me to devote my life to working for peace with justice.

Radical Discipleship

Our personal testimonies hopefully demonstrate a deepening of our faith in Christ in which evangelism, compassion, peace, justice, and reconciliation have become non-negotiables. Our stories, along with many others who have been influenced by Ron's life work, attest to his core commitment – namely, biblical discipleship and its radical implications. Ron has been labelled a social progressive in the media, and this label is not altogether untrue. However, as progressive as he may be, certain uncompromising evangelical commitments, such as the lordship of Christ and the final authority of Scripture, have defined him just as much. For him, it is about following Jesus faithfully and uncompromisingly.

We believe that the church needs to embrace radical discipleship in Christ today more than ever before. At least two striking reasons readily come to mind. First, despite the death knell of Christendom being trumpeted by many, the illegitimate marriage between patriotism and the gospel has only gotten stronger. Indeed, the cry to return to a Christian America has been shrieking louder than ever before. Something needs to counter this cry – a word of truth concerning authentic, biblical discipleship for those who have ears to listen needs to be proclaimed humbly but boldly.

And second, if Christian nationalism is a misguided form of discipleship, then 'virtual church' in the Internet age is a shallow form that also needs to be challenged. In the Facebook, Twitter, and texting generation (the average teenager sends 3,339 texts a month), the exchange of information and knowledge seems to be predicated on the principle of quantity over quality, width over depth. Consequently, we know so much and yet so little. The faith experience can also suffer these same consequences. This is not so much a critique of social media, indeed we have been willing and eager participants, as it is an acknowledgement of the need for a type of discipleship that requires deep biblical wisdom, human community and hands-on mission.

Radical discipleship – where evangelism, justice and reconciliation meet, where loyalty to Christ is stronger than loyalty to country, and where deep human community and wisdom reside – will be Ron Sider's enduring legacy.

FURTHER READING (ALL BY RON SIDER)

Rich Christians in Age of Hunger (2005) new ed. Nashville, TN: Thomas Nelson.
Completely Pro-Life (1986) Downers Grove, IL: IVP.
With Philip Olson and Heidi Unruh (2002) *Churches That Make a Difference* Grand Rapids, MI: Baker.
Scandal of Evangelical Conscience (2005) Grand Rapids, MI: Baker.
Just Generosity (2007) rev ed. Grand Rapids, MI: Baker.
I Am Not a Social Activist (2008) Scottdale, PA: Herald.
Just Politics (2012) Grand Rapids, MI: Baker.

CONCLUSION

Through the pages of this book readers have gained a glimpse into the lives of seven men and one woman who served as catalysts of transformational mission. These eight followers of Jesus are but a small selection of many others, across the world, both past and present, who have acknowledged Jesus as Lord and sought to live in faithful response to God's love in service to their fellow men and women in every walk of life.

The eight portrayed here are similar in a number of ways. Firstly, they all centred their lives on Jesus Christ. These are men and a woman whose submission to Christ as Lord of their lives and of history, of the personal and the social, of the cross and the empty tomb, was at the heart of their lives and ministries. They lived what they preached and preached what they lived as followers of Jesus. They were not interested in building their own kingdoms, but rather in building and making known the Kingdom of the King who rules by washing his disciples' feet.

They all engaged with the world rather than seeking to escape from it. They considered themselves sent into the world as Jesus was. So they did not wash their hands of the world's problems, but instead got their hands dirty in Christ's service. Through word and deed, and according to the gifts of the Spirit and the calling granted to each of them, they engaged in different realms of life as witnesses of God's love.

They differed in nationality, in family and social background, and in education. They grew up and worked in very different socio-political arenas. None of them denied their roots, but neither did they bind themselves to them: their concern for others stretched them far beyond their origins. Some of them wrote extensively and others promoted new writers. All of them had an eye for the poor and the disadvantaged, even if some walked from time to time with presidents and queens. For John Stott, the university campuses of the world were a key platform for his work. Kwame Bediako became Mr African Theology. David Gitari engaged deeply in the political life of Kenya. Catharine Padilla, Juan José Barreda and David Bussau invested themselves, their time and money in the poor in some of the major cities in the world. Peter Kuzmic and Ron Sider, like the others, believed firmly in biblical discipleship and its radical implications.

Many of them were key players in the 1974 Lausanne Congress and in the movement that brought together theologian practitioners from around the world, during the 1980s, as the International Fellowship of Evangelical Mission Theologians (INFEMIT), which, in turn, gave birth to the Oxford Centre for Mission Studies.

They shared and inspired in others the values of simplicity, austerity and appreciation for the beauties of life in addition to their love for the Word of God and their passion to link that Word to the world in which they lived.

Some of these catalysts of transformation have gone before us; some continue their work. As new generations of followers of Christ wrestle with the challenges of our day, and avail ourselves to serve as humble agents of God's mission, we pray that we too may recognize ourselves sent into the world as Jesus was and so carry forward the torch these followers of Jesus are passing on.

We bear the torch that flaming
Fell from the hands of those
Who gave their lives proclaiming
That Jesus died and rose
Ours is the same commission
The same glad message ours
Fired by the same ambition
To Thee we yield our powers

O Father who sustained them
O Spirit who inspired
Saviour, whose love constrained them
To toil with zeal untired
From cowardice defend us
From lethargy awake!
Forth on Thine errands send us
To labour for Thy sake.[15]

ENDNOTES

[1] Quote in Paddy Benson 2009:109, in Knighton (2009) ed. *Religion and Politics in Kenya: Essays in Honour of a Meddlesome Priest.* Basingstoke: Palgrave Macmillan.
[2] The account about David's life presented in this paper is taken from Tyndale's *Do Not Look Back, 2004.*
[3] Tyndale, p.16.
[4] Al, who was CEO of Bristol Myers, left his high-flying job and established the Institute for International Development Incorporated in (IIDI) in 1971, in order to help micro-entrepreneurs with working capital, in response to the need he saw in Bogota, Colombia, where IIDI gave its first loan.
[5] http://www.wtrc-tmed.org
[6] Australia's 10 Most Creative Minds, Order of Australia Medal, Ernst Young Social Entrepreneur of the Year Award, The first Social Entrepreneur to be inducted into the World Entrepreneur of the Year Academy in Monte Carlo, Australian of the Year Finalist, Special Humanitarian Award (Singapore), Hilton Distinguished Entrepreneur of the Year Award (USA), Australian Council for International Development: Sir Ron Wilson Human Rights Award, Beta Gamma Sigma Medallion for Entrepreneurship (USA), Senior Australian of the Year Award and Asia CEO Non-profit Leadership Team of the Year Finalist (Philippines).
[7] Some of these include: Bussau, D. (1998), Bussau, D., & Russ, M. (2000), Bussau, D., & Samuel, V. (1998), Bussau, D., & Getu, M. (2003).
[8] Bussau, paper on leadership.
[9] Ibid.
[10] Ibid.
[11] David commissioned two consultants to travel to DPRK and undertake a market research on the basis of which Maranatha Truest established a micro-enterprise development programme in partnership with the Government of North Korea.
[12] Op.cit.
[13] Adapted from Al Tizon and Paul Alexander (eds.) *Following Jesus: Essays on Radical Discipleship in Honor of Ronald J. Sider.* Oxford: Regnum Books, forthcoming 2013.
[14] Ronald J. Sider, *Good News and Good Works.* Grand Rapids, MI: Baker, 1999, 18.
[15] Written by Frank Houghton in 1930 © Copyright OMF.

